Literature in Perspective

W. B. Yeats

Raymond Cowell

Evans Brothers Limited London

Published by Evans Brothers Limited
Montague House, Russell Square, London, W.C.1
© Raymond Cowell 1969
First published 1969
Third printing 1976

Set in 11 on 12 point Bembo and printed in Great Britain by
The Garden City Press Limited, Letchworth, Hertfordshire SG6 1JS

ISBN 0 237 44411 9 cased   PRA 4885

ISBN 0 237 44439 9 limp

Literature in Perspective

Of recent years, the ordinary man who reads for pleasure has been gradually excluded from that great debate in which every intelligent reader of the classics takes part. There are two reasons for this: first, so much criticism floods from the world's presses that no one but a scholar living entirely among books can hope to read it all; and second, the critics and analysts, mostly academics, use a language that only their fellows in the same discipline can understand.

Consequently criticism, which should be as 'inevitable as breathing'—an activity for which we are all qualified—has become the private field of a few warring factions who shout their unintelligible battle cries to each other but make little communication to the common man.

Literature in Perspective aims at giving a straightforward account of literature and of writers—straightforward both in content and in language. Critical jargon is as far as possible avoided; any terms that must be used are explained simply; and the constant preoccupation of the authors of the Series is to be lucid.

It is our hope that each book will be easily understood, that it will adequately describe its subject without pretentiousness, so that the intelligent reader who wants to know about Donne or Yeats or Shakespeare will find enough in it to bring him up to date on critical estimates.

Even those who are well read, we believe, can benefit from a lucid exposition of what they may have taken for granted, and perhaps—dare it be said?—not fully understood.

K. H. G.

W. B. Yeats

Although Yeats's greatness as a poet is now widely accepted, there are several odd facts about his contemporary reputation and status. Perhaps the oddest is that, though he is granted the label of 'great' by many, attempts to demonstrate his greatness and its nature seem to concentrate on a handful of his poems, his anthology pieces. Thus his early and late work tends to be ignored, and the nature of his personal and poetic development becomes blurred. Again, his distinctive vocabulary—'perne', 'gyre', 'anti-self' and the rest—is treated either with erudite reverence or embarrassed apologies, as if these words were not a great deal more obvious in their meaning than the vocabulary of, say, Hopkins or Dylan Thomas. Similarly, his 'system' as expressed in *A Vision*—and as reflected in some of his poems—tends to be either quoted extensively and often irrelevantly throughout critical works or ignored completely. The result of all this is the prevalent idea of his 'difficulty', the fallacy that if one is to read him with any degree of success one needs a comprehensive knowledge of Irish history, occult speculation, Gaelic symbolism, 'and the Lord knows what!' The knowledge needed for a deep understanding of Yeats is knowledge about the kind of man he was, and is by no means esoteric.

This study of Yeats begins from the assumption that Yeats is a great poet in the Wordsworthian sense, 'a man talking to men', and that the sources of his genius are by no means as recondite as is sometimes suggested. It shows that Yeats was a seeker after truth who learned most in his search from his friends, and that the impetus for his constant development came from his faculty for deep, but constructive, self-criticism.

This, of course, is not to deny that Yeats's poetry makes considerable demands on the mind as well as the heart of the reader. It certainly does, and it is, perhaps, because of these demands that the peripheral questions arising from his poetry have received disproportionate attention, so that much remains to be said about his poetry *as* poetry.

I have indicated my critical debts in the reading list. More personal debts are to Mr. Kenneth Grose for his very helpful comments, to the pupils and students who have talked about Yeats with me in the past few years, and to my wife for her encouragement and patience.

R. C.

Contents

The Author

Raymond Cowell, B.A., Ph.D., is Dean of the Faculty of Humanities, Sunderland Polytechnic.

Acknowledgements

The author and publishers are indebted to M. B. Yeats and Macmillan & Co. Ltd, London, for permission to quote from the poetry and prose of W. B. Yeats. The USA rights are as follows: the extracts from *Collected Poems* by W. B. Yeats are reprinted with permission of The Macmillan Company, New York. Copyright 1903, 1906, 1907, 1912, 1916, 1918, 1919, 1924, 1928, 1931, 1933, 1934, 1935, 1940, 1944, 1945, 1946, 1950, 1956, by The Macmillan Company. Copyright 1940 by Georgie Yeats. Copyright renewed by William Butler Yeats 1931, 1934, 1935. Copyright renewed by Bertha Georgie Yeats 1940, 1944, 1945, 1946, 1952, 1961, 1962. Copyright renewed by Georgie Yeats 1956. The extracts from *Autobiography* by W. B. Yeats are reprinted with permission of The Macmillan Company. Copyright 1916, 1936 by The Macmillan Company, renewed 1944 by Bertha Georgie Yeats. The extracts from *Essays and Introductions* by W. B. Yeats are reprinted with permission of The Macmillan Company © Mrs. W. B. Yeats 1961. The extracts from *A Vision* by W. B. Yeats are reprinted with permission of The Macmillan Company. Copyright 1937 by The Macmillan Company, renewed 1955 by Bertha Georgie Yeats and Anne Butler Yeats. The extracts from *The Letters of W. B. Yeats*, edited by Alan Wade, are reprinted with permission of The Macmillan Company. Copyright 1953, 1954 by Anne Butler Yeats. The extracts from *Exploration* by W. B. Yeats are reprinted with permission of The Macmillan Company. Copyright © Mrs. W. B. Yeats 1962. The extract from 'In Memory of W. B. Yeats' from *Collected Shorter Poems 1927–1957*, by W. H. Auden is reprinted with permission of Faber & Faber Ltd and Random House Inc.; the extract from *The Identity of W. B. Yeats*, by Richard Ellmann, is reprinted with permission of Faber & Faber Ltd.

The photogravure of William Butler Yeats, 1908, by Alvin Langdon Coburn, on the cover, is reproduced by courtesy of George Eastman House. The drawing of Maude Gonne, by Sean O'Sullivan, is reproduced

If this is compared with another poem centred on his worries about his relationship with Maud, *The White Birds*, written a year earlier, it becomes clear that Yeats is beginning to realise how unsatisfactory dreams are as an escape from disturbing personal issues:

> Soon far from the rose and lily and fret of the flames would we be,
> Were we only white birds, my beloved, buoyed out on the foam of
> the sea!

These are the final lines of the poem, and they simply repeat what has gone before. In *The White Birds* there is no development through exploration of the central emotion, so that the style becomes repetitiously decorative, whereas in *The Two Trees* the conflict which inspires the poem gives it a continuing impetus.

The Lake Isle of Innisfree, whose genesis has already been described, appears in *The Rose*. In a sense this is another poem of escape, but at least the conflict between where he is and where he wants to be is actually present in the poem. The sheer beauty of the language—'the bee-loud glade', 'evening full of the linnet's wings'—conveys the intensity of his desire to get away from 'the pavements grey' of the city. True, Innisfree looms much larger than London in the poem, but without 'the pavements grey' it would be a much poorer poem. What Coleridge called 'the opposite and discordant qualities', both of thought and emotion, which can be fused through the efforts of the poetic Imagination, are at least present, if not yet as powerfully present as in his later poetry. The poem is perhaps typical of the whole volume. *The Rose* cannot be called a success, for the emotions are too often blurred by inexact imagery and predictable rhythms, as in *The White Birds*, but it is clearly the work of a developing poet, one who, though not perhaps knowing where he is going, recognises that progress and experiment are essential.

By 1894 Yeats was something of a celebrity in London, perhaps even a 'character': he always exaggerated his Irishness when in London, and his English tastes when in Dublin. In 1894, too, he met 'Diana Vernon'—to use the false name he discreetly gave her—and began a relationship which led to their living together for a time in 1896. He never succeeded in convincing himself that she could take the place of Maud in his affections, however, and indeed Yeats spent some time in Paris, in 1894, partly in the hope of persuading Maud to marry him. Though unsuccessful in this aim, he did meet the French poet Verlaine, whom he greatly admired. Verlaine, in a poem on the art of poetry, had urged fellow writers: 'Grab eloquence and wring its neck' ('*Prends l'éloquence et tords lui le cou*'), and one can therefore safely assume that by talking to him Yeats strengthened his growing suspicion of high-flown eloquence, verbal decoration and—one of his favourite words of abuse—'rhetoric'. Throughout Paris, the 'aestheticism' of the Nineties was at its height, the belief in 'art for art's sake', in artistic beauty as an end in itself which need have no reference to ordinary life. The play *Axel* by Count Villiers de l'Isle Adam, which Yeats admired so much that he read it painfully in the original, expressed this view of art and life very succinctly in the famous line: 'As for living, our servants will do that for us.' After his stay in Paris, Yeats returned to Sligo for several months, feeling depressed and unsettled. Prompted largely by these feelings, perhaps, Yeats here began to explore other aspects of the occult, with the help of Mary Battle, and—much more important—to prepare for publication *Poems* of 1895, which was to contain all that he wished to preserve from his early work. This task obviously involved Yeats, always his own severest critic, in deep and often discouraging thought about the aims of his poetry. 1894 and 1895, then, were years of literary and personal uncertainty for Yeats, but he emerged from them with a clearer sense of purpose. Early in 1896 Yeats settled in Woburn Buildings, Bloomsbury, where he was to live, on and off, for twenty-four years.

It was in 1896, while he was in Ireland with Arthur Symons, that he visited Lady Gregory, whom he had met briefly before, at her ancestral home, Coole Park, and there is a great deal of truth in what Yeats says of her immediate influence on him: 'She brought to my wavering thoughts steadfast nobility.' He was searching for new directions, and she, the embodiment of the traditions of the Irish Protestant aristocracy, set him thinking, by word and example, about the contribution these traditions could make to Irish life, and indeed to life in general. Like Maud Gonne and John O'Leary before her, she entered Yeats's life at just the right moment. Professor Stock has put this point very well:

> It was his luck, or his talent, to dream of fine things and then wake and discover them—to conceive heroic simplicity and make a friend of John O'Leary; legendary beauty and find Maud Gonne at his door; a tradition of nobility and be made at home in Coole Park.
> W. B. YEATS, HIS POETRY AND THOUGHT

Though Symons was suspicious, thinking that Lady Gregory was out to 'get Willie' as a mere protégé, Yeats, who knew a little of the Irish Great House tradition through an earlier friendship with the Ormsby-Gore family of Sligo, responded eagerly to her friendship. Seeing that he needed money and advice, Lady Gregory, a wealthy widow, gave him both. The idea she proposed to Yeats with particular enthusiasm was that of an Irish National Theatre with the aim of restoring, through drama, Ireland's 'national identity'. The idea was not, of course, new to Yeats, but Lady Gregory made it a real possibility for the first time. These plans were strengthened by Yeats's meeting with the Irish dramatist, John Millington Synge, in Paris in 1896. Synge's influence on Yeats, and Yeats's on him, were to go far beyond literature, but for the moment a nucleus of enthusiasts was forming. George Moore and Edward Martyn, whom Yeats had met previously, joined with him, Synge and Lady Gregory in 1896 to start thinking seriously about a national theatre.

The result of their efforts, the Abbey Theatre, was still seven years away, however, and these years were to be among the most important in the whole of Yeats's poetic career. As always, his social and political opinions were developing concurrently with his personal, literary and philosophical views. His association with O'Leary and with the Irish Republican Brotherhood was now much closer. Political unrest in Dublin was growing yearly. There were riots, in which Maud Gonne played a prominent part, in connection with certain restrictions for the Jubilee of

Queen Victoria. His social views, on the other hand, were changing too. He spent a large part of 1897 convalescing with Lady Gregory at Coole Park, and through conversations with her he began to think of society as comprising, essentially, three groups, the hereditary landed nobility, the peasant class and the commercial middle class. The first two groups were, they decided, a fit audience for poetry, while the third was the enemy of any kind of artistic enterprise. These views on an audience for his poetry stayed with Yeats, pretty well unmodified, throughout his career. Always in his mind, apart from these political and social views, was his love for Maud, though he was beginning to recognise, sporadically, that Maud would never marry him: 'My devotion might as well have been offered to an image in a milliner's window, or to a statue in a museum.'

Though very powerful, these new influences did not colour his emotional being immediately, so that his next volume of poetry, *The Wind among the Reeds* of 1899, comes as something of a disappointment unless one bears in mind the emotional and intellectual wrench involved in changing the habits of ten years and more. The volume is appropriately dated in 1899 for it is Yeats's final complete expression of views with which he was already intellectually dissatisfied. This is not to say, of course, that Yeats changes completely after this volume—there are traces of the early Yeats throughout almost all his work—but after this he is always consciously trying to develop. Many of the poems in the volume are clearly the products of acute depression, and they are often self-indulgent and highly-stylised, mannered verbal tapestries of languorous lovers and pale maidens with golden tresses and pearl-pale hands. Writing of this time in *Autobiographies*, he recalls that he felt: 'I must some day become difficult and obscure.' This sounds rather perverse at first, but it is simply a recognition on Yeats's part that the world is a difficult and complex place and that his poetry has been evading or simplifying its problems. He was beginning to feel that his revulsion against realism and science had been naïvely extreme and had involved the exclusion of much that the poet should be struggling to make sense of. As he put in *The Tree of Life*, an essay of this time: 'We should ascend out of common life, the thoughts of the newspapers, of the market place, of men of science, but only so far as we can carry the normal, passionate, reasoning self, the personality as a whole.' Though still rejecting vehemently Arnold's famous assertion that all great poetry is in essence 'a criticism of life', he no longer felt that it could profitably be a dream. Though the atmosphere of this volume is still that of what has come to be called disparagingly the 'Celtic Twilight', difficulty and 'obscurity' are very much in Yeats's thoughts.

It is a volume of drifting moods. The poem actually called *The Moods* is typical of the volume's strengths and weaknesses:

> Time drops in decay,
> Like a candle burnt out,
> And the mountains and woods
> Have their day, have their day;
> What one in the rout
> Of the fire-born moods
> Has fallen away?

The weakly rhetorical question, the self-consciously plangent repetition, the imperfect cadence midway and the lack of any rhythmic variation, point to a certain complacency in the attitudes of world-weary knowledge. A fixed poetic attitude is being rather lazily embellished. Traces of a real or unpleasant world, when they find their way into this volume, are seen as intrusions, as in these lines from *The Lover Tells of the Rose in his Heart*:

> All things uncomely and broken, all things worn out and old,
> The cry of a child by the roadway, the creak of a lumbering cart,
> The heavy steps of the ploughman, splashing the wintry mould,
> Are wronging your image that blossoms a rose in the deeps of my
> heart.

One might say, using the terms of his later poetry, that 'things uncomely and broken' are the 'unpurged images' that are to press into the world of pure, 'masterful' images much more urgently in future years. In spite of its predominantly escapist tone, however, the volume does recognise the existence of threats to perfect love, such as the bigotry of slanderous tongues; and the conclusion of one poem, at least, strikes a characteristic Yeatsian note of personal and dramatic testiness:

> O beast of the wilderness, bird of the air,
> Must I endure your amorous cries?

HE THINKS OF HIS PAST GREATNESS

Yet on the whole such themes as the immortality conferred by great literature, and regret for a past era of heroic simplicity, predominate. It is symptomatic of the artificiality of this world that the poet is frequently referred to in the third person. Typical of the extremely rarified atmosphere of some of the poems is *He Wishes his Beloved were Dead*, in which a lover wishes his loved one were dead so that they might be spared the irksome physical separation which is part of ordinary life:

> O would, beloved, that you lay
> Under the dock-leaves in the ground,
> While lights were paling one by one.

The complete unreality of the poem's central idea makes even the delicate beauty of the imagery and rhythm seem insipid. In fact, one's chief emotion on reading this volume is frustration; there is obviously outstanding poetic ability here, but it is linked so tenuously to reality. It is not surprising that some of the more perceptive contemporary critics were beginning to wonder when he would move on to something new. One such criticism came from W. K. Magee (pseudonym John Eglington): 'he looks too much away from himself and from his age, does not feel the facts of life enough, but seeks in art an escape from them.' This stung Yeats, and he replied, unsatisfactorily, in the Dublin *Daily Express*, saying that poetry was 'a revelation of a hidden life' and need not concern itself with anything apart from this hidden life. A possible cause of the stubborn escapism and idealism of this poetry was, perhaps, his refusal to accept finally that Maud Gonne would never marry him. He still fought against the idea, and followed her about England and France, proposing at the slightest opportunity. She was, however, becoming more and more intimately involved in politics, and proportionately less interested in Yeats. Her attitude towards him took a long time to sink into his personality.

Between 1899 and 1902 Yeats was preoccupied with early plans for the revival of the Irish theatre, which culminated in the formation of the Irish National Dramatic Society in 1902. The society aimed to present Irish plays with Irish actors and thus form a rallying-point for the political and cultural aspirations of the Irish nation. Thus, Yeats's intensely patriotic play, *Cathleen ni Houlihan*, was produced by the society in 1902 with Maud in the leading role. It is an allegorical story of how an old woman leads a young man away from friends and home to a life of hardship, which he endures for Ireland's sake. At the end of the play, after the man has proved himself a worthy Irish patriot, the old woman is transformed into a beautiful girl. The clear political message, that Ireland could become beautiful and noble again only through self-sacrifice, was obviously an incendiary one at that time. For example, the accession of Edward VII in 1902 had provoked further riots in Dublin. It was to remain a popular play with the Irish audiences; and indeed in old age, thinking about this play, Yeats asked (though soon dismissing the possibility): 'Did that play of mine send out/Certain men the English shot?' One personal motive for the play was obviously to please Maud Gonne, to make her think differently of him, but he was unsuccessful in that aim and in 1903 learned by telegram that Maud had married an Irish patriot, John MacBride, and had become a Catholic. Though one can see why MacBride appealed to her—he had led an Irish Brigade in the Boer War, and was known for his revolutionary sentiments—those who knew the couple thought it a strange match, for MacBride had none of Maud's artistic tastes or sensibility. Yeats's reaction, it goes without saying, was deep disappointment, although he remained devoted to Maud even now, and when she left MacBride two years later he defended her angrily against public denunciations. Indeed, the Dublin middle classes' treatment of Maud, and later of Synge's plays, confirmed him in the aristocratic social views he had formed in conversations with Lady Gregory.

The next year, 1904, was a very eventful one for Yeats. In December the Abbey Theatre presented its first programme of plays, by Yeats, Synge and Lady Gregory, and *In the Seven Woods* was arousing strong reactions. The title refers to the seven woods of Coole Park, and this in itself shows how decisive Lady Gregory's influence had been in the writing of this volume. It is a crucial point in his poetic career, for here he finally speaks with his own voice, expressing, at this time, considerable bitterness and disillusionment. Such influences of his earlier years as aestheticism, Pater's ideas, Verlaine, occult speculation, and the many others, are here either assimilated into a distinctively Yeatsian utterance or shed completely. Sadly, but perhaps predictably in view of the generally rigid contemporary notions about what poetry should be, this volume was comparatively unpopular.

In this volume the weariness and revulsion which had often been a fashionable affectation in his earlier poetry are palpable in every aspect of the writing, perhaps particularly in the tone and imagery. The new directness and subtlety of style are prefigured in the title itself. The year 1903 saw, as well as Maud Gonne's marriage, great storms, and many of the trees in Lady Gregory's estate were uprooted; the feeling of being uprooted lies behind many of the poems in the volume. The word 'bitterness' occurs in the title poem, which is about the accession of Edward, 'new commonness upon the throne', and the paper Coronation festoons which so disgust Yeats. Although in this poem Yeats finds some solace in the retreat offered by the woods, the bitterness, aristocratic in this poem, registers much too forcefully to be forgotten by the reader. Quite as intense as this social bitterness is the personal bitterness in such a poem as *Never Give all the Heart*. This is an outburst by a betrayed lover who has given all his love, without any reservations, to a woman who looks upon love as an elaborate game. 'Passionate women,' the man says with soured irony, shy away from total devotion:

> O never give the heart outright,
> For they, for all smooth lips can say,
> Have given their hearts up to the play.

And who could play it well enough
If deaf and dumb and blind with love?
He that made this knows all the cost,
For he gave all his heart and lost.

The rhythmic subtlety which places such a telling stress on 'he'
in the penultimate line, the suggestion of seething rage conveyed
by the cumulative rhythm of the previous two lines, the dis-
illusioned reference to the no longer ideal, but treacherous,
'smooth lips'—all these show the emergence of Yeats's distinctive
greatness. The same theme is treated, again very effectively, in
O do not love too long, but the greatest achievement of the
volume is undoubtedly *Adam's Curse*.

Maud Gonne later recalled the occasion of this poem. Before
he knew of her intention to marry MacBride, though already
suspecting that his love was rejected, Yeats had seen Maud,
dishevelled in a riding habit, after a typically busy day of political
business, and had remarked on the contrast between her com-
posed, well-dressed sister and Maud:

> I saw Willie Yeats looking critically at me and he told Kathleen
> he liked her dress and that she was looking younger than ever. It
> was on that occasion Kathleen remarked that it was hard work
> being beautiful, which Willie turned into his poem 'Adam's Curse'.
> Maud Gonne MacBride, A SERVANT OF THE QUEEN, p. 328

The poem is essentially a recognition of the immense difficulty
of achieving any kind of real or permanent beauty in view of our
flawed human state, Adam's curse. In the poem, pondering
Kathleen's remark, Yeats gropes towards the reason for the
failure of his love for Maud. His love, he sees, has been nourished
only on 'high courtesy', has taken too little notice of the real
world of pain and disappointment, and has thus been immensely
vulnerable in its innocence. The moon symbolises his love for
Maud, but by the end of the poem it has become 'hollow' and
'weary-hearted'. An apparently ideal love has proved illusory
because of its remoteness from life. Thus, in one sense, Yeats is
criticising himself for making the critical remarks remembered
by Maud; they betray his refusal to accept the fact that beauty

involves hard work, that love involves acceptance of a whole being. The tone of the opening lines is quietly conversational, the rhythm suggesting beautifully the easy, informal atmosphere:

> We sat together at one summer's end,
> That beautiful mild woman, your close friend,
> And you and I, and talked of poetry.

In the course of this conversation, the poet remarks that writing poetry is a thankless task, for, paradoxically, the poet's efforts are devoted to making the finished poems seem natural and effortless. Since the best poems give no evidence of the sheer hard work that has gone into their making, they win no praise from the mass of humanity, 'bankers, schoolmasters, and clergymen', who reserve their respect for the kind of hard work that shows. Maud's sister takes Yeats up on this point, and suggests that this is surely true of any kind of beauty:

> ... 'to be born woman is to know—
> Although they do not talk of it at school—
> That we must labour to be beautiful.'

The common sense and truth of this immediately strike Yeats, and he develops the idea, saying that love itself is often much more difficult than it appears at first sight. Any 'fine thing' demands much of a man. The group now lapses into silence, watching the moon:

> A moon, worn as if it had been a shell
> Washed by time's waters as they rose and fell
> About the stars and broke in days and years.

Suddenly all the general conversation focuses, in Yeats's mind, on Maud, and he realises how relevant all these thoughts are to his own despair; he has been trying to win a 'fine thing' without making the necessary sacrifice and effort:

> I had a thought for no one's but your ears:
> That you were beautiful, and that I strove
> To love you in the old high way of love;
> That it had all seemed happy, and yet we'd grown
> As weary-hearted as that hollow moon.

The long vowel sounds of this last line help to register with great force and finality Yeats's disappointment and regret; Yeats has realised, too late, how mistaken he has been in his attitude to Maud. The poem as a whole has the beautiful simplicity, the result of unobtrusive hard work, such as is mentioned within it. The colloquial vigour of the first line, for example, ensures that there is no trace of self-dramatisation here, and the language as a whole has the kind of simple inevitability that is the mark of the greatest poetry.

This volume contains fourteen poems and only one is specifically about Ireland, though this became very popular with the revolutionaries, *Red Hanrahan's Song about Ireland*. The tone of all the other poems is, to a greater or less degree, critical, wary, disappointed. *Under the Moon* explicitly states his disenchantment with the remote poetic worlds of myth and legend, 'lands that seem too dim to be burdens on the heart'. What he has learned in *Adam's Curse* makes him suspicious of escapism:

> Because of something told under the famished horn
> Of the hunter's moon, that hung between the night and the day,
> To dream of women whose beauty was folded in dismay,
> Even in an old story, is a burden not to be borne.

Absolutely typical of this new intellectual and emotional wariness, the unwillingness to consider anything less than the complete truth, however unpalatable, is *The Folly of being Comforted*. This is an explicit rejection of the consolatory sentiments, expressed to him in his disappointment, that his frustrated love will grow less bitter as the person who has rejected it loses her beauty. The poem is in the form of a dialogue, and the person who is trying to comfort Yeats concludes: 'all that you need is patience.' Yeats knows better, however; he knows that the beauty and nobility of the woman he loves will live on in spite of age. He knows he still loves her, and prefers to accept his disappointment and bitterness rather than distort his feelings for the sake of consolation:

> O heart! O heart! if she'd but turn her head,
> You'd know the folly of being comforted.

Here the colloquial contractions ('she'd', 'don't') suppress the initial suggestion of rhetoric, and Yeats's stubborn loyalty to his emotions is conveyed by these two clipped lines. Here is an early example of the combination of formal and colloquial diction and syntax which is typical of his later work.

Yeats was now in his late thirties, an established poet but a radically dissatisfied one, who was turning away from the literary establishment which had welcomed him. It is hardly surprising that most contemporary reviewers were puzzled, for with all the energy of a younger man Yeats was beginning to explore fresh possibilities. *In the Seven Woods*, being the first of several changes of direction in his poetic career, would be even more puzzling than the later ones. It would not be true to say that Yeats was starting again, for there was in his earlier poetry an element of urgency and directness which often threatened to burst the fragile moulds Yeats was using. His disappointment in love, his new friendships, his consuming interest in the idea of a National Theatre, were all driving him in a new direction. He had left behind him, perhaps, the extreme confusion of the period between 1896 and 1900, and he was determined to widen his mind and art. Between 1902 and 1908, partly because of his involvement with the Abbey Theatre but also because of his artistic dissatisfaction with his capabilities, he wrote only one lyric, *O do not love too long*. He was beginning the process of 'remaking' himself that was to occupy him for the remaining thirty-seven years of his life. The process, however, was one of constant modification rather than radical reorientation, and the earlier works considered in this chapter show clearly both why he was dissatisfied and why he felt the confidence to explore new possibilities.

2

Towards Modernism: 1903–1914

This chapter will deal with Yeats's life, poetry and thought up to *Responsibilities* of 1914, a collection which shows clearly how deeply he had thought about poetry and his life in the vital years from 1903 to 1914. Like all of Yeats's important volumes, it is both an end and a beginning, but *Responsibilities* is chiefly remarkable for the decisive stylistic development it reveals. Although the development towards the controlled fury and energy of his mature poetry was a slow and difficult one, this volume shows quite clearly that Yeats is going to be a great modern poet. The characteristic Yeatsian temptations—aristocratic disdain, aesthetic or mystical remoteness, jewelled rhetoric, nostalgic romanticism —are still present in this period, but the resistance to them is increasingly honest, even heroic. Indeed he was never to leave these and related temptations completely behind him, for in a very important sense all Yeats's poetry is a poetry of temptation. Such diverse influences as those of Pound, Synge, his work with the Abbey Theatre, Swedenborg and, of course, Blake, went along with the central literary revelation of the period, the insight into Donne and the Metaphysicals, to make him see the temptations more clearly and search more hopefully for the alternatives.

In the early years of this period of his life, his friendship with Lady Gregory continued to sustain him, and from the work of Synge—for Synge and Yeats were never very close personally— he learned, as he says, to reject 'the holy city of the Imagination' and seek after an ideal relation between the Imagination and life. The Abbey Theatre opened in 1904, hoping to find, as its prospectus put it, 'an uncorrupted and imaginative audience, trained to listen by its passion for oratory'. Such hopes were finally crushed by the hissing reception given to Synge's *The Playboy of the Western World* in 1907, and though Yeats continued to harbour hopes for the theatre, the death of Synge in 1909, and increasingly determined attempts by the sponsors to interfere with artistic policy, led him to resign his managership in 1910. Before then, in 1909, with his gift for fruitful friendship, Yeats had met Ezra Pound, another influence to learn from and, more important, to kick against.

Yeats's contempt for the common people at this time in his life is, if not easily defensible, at least understandable. The Abbey Theatre audience had hissed Maud Gonne in 1905, after she had left her husband; and Lady Gregory's nephew, Hugh Lane, had his generous offer to give a collection of modern French paintings to Dublin Corporation rejected because the Corporation would not agree to house them in the kind of gallery Lane thought they deserved. This led Lane to leave the pictures to the London National Gallery, which in turn led, on his death in 1915, to an unpleasant legal wrangle as to whose the pictures really were, centring on an unwitnessed codicil to Lane's will bequeathing the pictures to the Dublin Gallery on condition that within five years of his death a suitable gallery was found for them. Yeats saw this affair as a slight to both Lane and Lady Gregory and an indication of the impossibility of wise democratic government. These anti-democratic views were strengthened in 1907 by his reading of Castiglione's *The Courtier*, an Italian Renaissance outline of the virtues of an aristocratic way of life, which Yeats considered 'one of the great books of our civilisation'. Such a poem as *September 1913* reflects these anti-democratic feelings. On the whole, Yeats tried to remain aloof from public affairs in these years, to 'be secret and exult', but the very contempt of some of his anti-democratic poems reveals his unadmitted need for a wider audience than his literary and aristocratic friends could provide.

These feelings about contemporary Dublin find their way into Yeats's poetry of this period, but his poetry never becomes merely a receptacle for his personal and social opinions. His

point of forming the Ulster Volunteers. Yeats expresses his feelings in two letters of May 1916 to Lady Gregory in which he says he feels that the work of years has been overthrown—he is probably thinking of his own efforts to separate poetry and politics, as stated in *On being Asked for a War Poem* of February 1915—and admits: 'I had no idea that any public event could so deeply move me.' His poetic expression of his reactions, *Easter 1916*, was withheld from the general public (though read to Maud Gonne, who thought it 'inadequate'), and printed only in a very limited edition for friends.

The years between 1914 and 1917 (when *The Wild Swans at Coole* was first published by Yeats's sister's Cuala Press, though some poems were added later) were important ones in Yeats's life. For example, the Lane affair, and his exasperation over it, reached a climax when Lane was drowned in the *Lusitania* in 1915. In the same year he refused a knighthood. Apart from this, he proposed again to Maud, and was rejected again, and then to her adopted niece, Iseult, who also refused him. Eventually, in October 1917, he married Miss Georgie Hyde-Lees, whom he had first met in 1911, and with whom, as he says in *Under Saturn*, he was to be very happy. His attempts to formulate his astrological and occult speculations into a 'system' also date from this time, for his wife had the gift of 'automatic writing', a fact which delighted Yeats. However, although these were decisive and formative years for Yeats, *The Wild Swans at Coole* contains few contemporary references and is absolutely silent about the Easter Rising. There is a marked continuity between *Responsibilities* and this volume, which is hardly surprising if we consider the vast problems on which Yeats had embarked in the earlier volume. In view of this continuity it is understandable that one reviewer, John Middleton Murry, in a now famous review, said that Yeats's inspiration was exhausted, that he was now simply repeating himself, having nothing new to say: 'he has the apparatus of enchantment but no potency in his soul.' With the benefit of hindsight, we can see that Yeats, with characteristic thoroughness, was rethinking earlier pre-occupations.

Indeed it is this very subject, the exhaustion of his imaginative powers with age, which Yeats considers in the title poem. His intensive reading of Wordsworth in 1916 certainly contributes to this poem, written in October of that year, but this Wordsworthian theme was to be given a distinctively Yeatsian colouring in several poems of this volume. In *The Wild Swans at Coole* age is seen as an almost physical assault upon his youthful imaginative energy:

> The nineteenth autumn has come upon me
> Since I first made my count.

Yeats reflects that he has now been delighting each summer in the beauty of the Coole swans for nineteen years, and his habit of counting them each year now reminds him unpleasantly of his own age. He senses acutely and painfully that a gap is opening up between himself and timeless Nature:

> Their hearts have not grown old;
> Passion or conquest, wander where they will,
> Attend upon them still.

The word 'attend' reminds one of the poem of old age, *The Spur*, of twenty years later, where 'lust and rage . . . dance attention upon his old age', but in 1916 Yeats was not ready to accept such alternatives to the traditional sources of poetic Imagination, and this poem ends with the fear that one day, the swans, symbolising his creative relationship with Nature, will have gone, leaving him desolate:

> Among what rushes will they build,
> By what lake's edge or pool
> Delight men's eyes when I awake some day
> To find they have flown away?

Within the poem, the urgency of the theme of the passing both of time and imaginative energy is suggested through sudden changes of tense:

> The nineteenth autumn has come upon me
> Since I first made my count;
> I saw, before I had well finished,
> All suddenly mount

> And scatter wheeling in great broken rings
> Upon their clamorous wings.

The perfect tense of the opening line contrasts with the present tenses of the previous stanza, and the change in this stanza from 'has' to 'had' conveys an almost brutal finality in the swans' premature departure. And always, behind this Yeatsian poem, is a poignant Wordsworthian resonance, as in the line, 'Trod with a lighter tread', which recalls, perhaps, 'like a roe/I bounded o'er the mountains' of *Tintern Abbey*.

However, Yeats could not be satisfied with the Wordsworthian 'still, sad music of humanity', and in the next poem in the volume, *In Memory of Major Robert Gregory*, he suggests a contrast which is quite outside the Wordsworthian experience, that between ways of living, intensely or lethargically, which makes the passing of time, and indeed the very fact of death itself, seem irrelevant:

> Some burn damp faggots, others may consume
> The entire combustible world in one small room
> As though dried straw, and if we turn about
> The bare chimney is gone black out
> Because the work had finished in that flare.

Life as a short, intense flare is the theme of this elegy for Lady Gregory's son, who was killed in action over Italy in 1918. The poem begins as a meditation on death. Yeats remembers three completely different types of men, Lionel Johnson, John Synge, and his uncle, George Pollexfen, and thought about their deaths leads him to a sense of deprivation and solitude, for they were 'a portion of my mind and life'. Then, however, the poem changes direction as Yeats turns his attention to a more recent and different death, that of Major Gregory. Whereas the other deaths depressed Yeats, this one, he says, has a different effect, one that goes beyond conventional elegiac tributes, the effect, almost, of tragic joy. The stanzas which record Yeats's sense of his own and society's loss, and suggest his response to the facts, lie at the heart of the poem's meaning:

> We dreamed that a great painter had been born
> To cold Clare rock and Galway rock and thorn,
> To that stern colour and that delicate line
> That are our secret discipline
> Wherein the gazing heart doubles her might.
> Soldier, scholar, horseman, he,
> And yet he had the intensity
> To have published all to be a world's delight.
>
> What other could so well have counselled us
> In all lovely intricacies of a house
> As he that practised or that understood
> All work in metal or in wood,
> In moulded plaster or in carven stone?
> Soldier, scholar, horseman, he,
> And all he did done perfectly
> As though he had but that one trade alone.

The key-word here is 'intensity', and 'cold' and 'stern' relate to this word to present the kind of artist or writer Yeats admired most, one combining passion and detachment. The repeated 'all' of the second stanza conveys the universality of his gifts and the tragedy of his loss. After these stanzas, the elegiac tone changes to one of self-rebuke, as Yeats tells himself that in his brief life Gregory had fulfilled himself, had become 'life's epitome' through his heroic attitude to art and life, so that mere physical duration would have been almost an anti-climax: 'What made us dream that he could comb grey hair?' Meditating on Gregory's life and death, Yeats comes to see that, through intensity, one can defeat time and death. In a sense, then, this poem makes the worries of *The Wild Swans at Coole* momentarily superfluous; there is an alternative to burning damp faggots, to taking an annual stock of one's imaginative reserves, and that is to live intensely, 'consume/The entire combustible world in one small room'.

Viewed more superficially, this poem reflects Yeats's ever-increasing affection for Coole Park and the Gregory family. The strength of this affection is obvious in the, at first sight, astonishing suggestion that Robert Gregory's life was superior to, more meaningful than, Synge's and Johnson's. Clearly Robert Gregory here symbolises a style of life and art, rooted in the aristocratic way of life, that Yeats admired: there is nothing in what survives of his art, or what we know of his life, to provide a literal justification of Yeats's lavish praise.

Like many of his greatest poems, *In Memory of Major Robert Gregory* contains the element of self-criticism, which serves, together with the rigid eight-line stanza scheme, to control and make articulate the poet's emotions. Another poem, again on the theme of age, makes the implied complacency of the title, *Men Improve with the Years*, the occasion of further self-rebuke. This poem, written in July 1916, concerns his attitude to Iseult Gonne. It begins by suggesting that his delight in her is purely aesthetic, but then he re-examines this view:

> And yet, and yet,
> Is this my dream, or the truth?
> O would that we had met
> When I had my burning youth!
> But I grow old among dreams,
> A weather-worn, marble triton
> Among the streams.

With characteristic honesty, Yeats rejects the temptation of self-deceiving complacency, and admits that he at least does not 'improve', in this odd sense of outgrowing passion, with the years. He still retains the burning intensity of his youth, though not youth itself.

In these poems, in spite of the sardonic escapism of *The Collar-Bone of a Hare*, Yeats is moving towards his central poetic theme, the intrinsic though not always obvious superiority of actual life, however confused, over any alternatives to, or substitutes for, life. The supreme quality of life is its intensity, and one example of this intensity, sexual love, is the subject of *Solomon to Sheba*. Always, in the poems of this period, the heart is the ultimate value, satisfied with nothing but 'a living beauty', and rejecting as inadequate such possible substitutes as 'beauty that is cast out of a mould/In bronze' (*The Living Beauty*). In this very line there is a close verbal anticipation of *Among School Children*, and the sentiments too, of course, recur in part of that poem. Again in anticipation of later poems, those on old age, Yeats asserts in this volume that age is not a physical but an emotional process:

> I thought no more was needed
> Youth to prolong
> Than dumb-bell and foil
> To keep the body young.
> *O who could have foretold*
> *That the heart grows old?*

A SONG

It is easy to fend off physical old age (Ezra Pound was teaching him to fence) but the fight against the insidious forces of emotional senility is much more difficult. The chief weapon in this fight is, of course, intensity—one is aware at this time of the continuing influence of Pater—and in *To a Young Beauty* he tells Iseult (who acted as his secretary in the summer of 1916) that only total dedication can achieve this intensity, in either life or art.

As Hugh Kenner has shown, this is one of the most carefully constructed of Yeats's volumes, and the juxtaposition of *To a Young Girl* and *The Scholars* is one of Yeats's finest strokes. The poet tells the young girl that he understands the intensity of her emotions; *he* remembers the intensity of youth, even though her mother has forgotten. The mother 'has forgot . . . the wild thought/That she denies', and similarly the scholars are 'forgetful of their sins', and so in dealing with literature they are as negative and repressive as the mother in dealing with life. Editing the words of literary texts, but impervious to the intense emotions that produced them, they miss the point, pathetically and absurdly:

> All shuffle there; all cough in ink;
> All wear the carpet with their shoes;
> All think what other people think;
> All know the man their neighbour knows.
> Lord, what would they say
> Did their Catullus walk that way?

58

This is one of the most scathing passages in literature, as scathing as Lucio's description of Angelo in *Measure for Measure* (Act I, Sc. 4), and rather similar in its line of attack. One detects the spirit of Pound's iconoclasm here, and it is a fact that he helped Yeats with this poem. The close similarity in theme between these two poems is almost obscured, on a first reading, by the widely different tones; the first one sympathetic and comforting, the second contemptuous and merciless. Physical death, and the kind of emotional death caused by intellectualism and the denial of the heart, are pervasive themes in the volume *The Wild Swans at Coole*; and in a fine rollicking ballad, *Tom O'Roughley*, the final insult to death is launched: 'What's dying but a second wind?' The most prominent influence behind this poem is the perennial one of Blake, whose poems often contain similar shock tactics to make the same points: 'An aimless joy is a pure joy'; 'And if my dearest friend were dead/I'd dance a measure on his grave.' This defiant gaiety in the face of death is very far removed from the gloomy apprehensions of the poem *The Wild Swans at Coole*, and quite close to the gaiety in the midst of suffering and desolation celebrated in *Lapis Lazuli* of 1936. Through these poems in the first part of *The Wild Swans at Coole*, Yeats develops a positive attitude to time, age and death, an attitude based on the primacy of the heart and the concept of intensity in art and life.

It seems likely that Yeats's formulation of these attitudes was helped by his marriage, from which arose a stronger sense of the distinctive value of feminine qualities. This fact is reflected in the increasingly important part played by women in his poetry of the next twenty years: Sheba and Crazy Jane, Mabel Beardsley, Iseult, Constance Markiewicz—apart from Lady Gregory and Maud Gonne—occur, some frequently, in this poetry.

The evolution of this positive attitude to life, which Yeats was continuing in this volume, necessarily involves for a poet as conscious of his audience as he was, constant changes in his relation to this audience, and in *The Fisherman* he presents the kind of man who, he thinks, would appreciate the intense, unadorned poetry he is trying to write:

> Maybe a twelvemonth since
> Suddenly I began,
> In scorn of this audience,
> Imagining a man,
> And his sun-freckled face,
> And grey Connemara cloth,
> Climbing up to a place
> Where stone is dark under froth,
> And the down-turn of his wrist
> When the flies drop in the stream;
> A man who does not exist,
> A man who is but a dream;
> And cried, 'Before I am old
> I shall have written him one
> Poem maybe as cold
> And passionate as the dawn.'

The recognition that this man does not exist is a brave one, for Yeats is desperate to find an alternative audience to 'the living men that I hate'. What this imaginary fisherman symbolises is an apparently detached intensity; fishing is an activity of quiet concentration, the absolute antithesis of the favourite pastime of Yeats's rejected audience, politics. The apparent paradox of the fisherman's intense detachment is paralleled by the cold passion of the poetry Yeats hope to write for him and his kind. Typically, the emotional equilibrium of wishful thinking stays with Yeats very briefly and in *The People*, written in January 1915, seven months after *The Fisherman*, Yeats is once again involved in doubts. In *The Fisherman* he had explicitly abandoned the idea of writing for his own race, but here, recalling his fierce arguments with Maud about the people, he goes a long way towards suggesting that his own detached analytical attitude to the people is inferior to the emotional, uncomplaining, realistic love that Maud feels for them. Yeats's argument with himself on this question of his relation to the people is to recur later in such a poem as *Meditations in Time of Civil War*.

The volume ends with a group of poems about the value of art. Since, as Yeats says in *On being Asked for a War Poem*, the poet has 'no gift to set a statesman right', what, then, can he achieve? *Upon a Dying Lady* explores some aspects of this question. It was written between 1912 and 1914 about Mabel Beardsley, the sister of one of the most extreme aesthetes of the Nineties, who was dying of cancer. In a letter to Lady Gregory, Yeats speaks of her and her brother's 'passion for reality', a passion achieved through the intensity of art. In the face of death, through art, not conventional religion, Mabel Beardsley is able to face up to reality gaily. Her artist friends surround her with drawings, dolls and happiness, and though, in the third section, the priest has his day on a religious festival, she takes most joy in the artists and their dolls. Having 'lived in joy' she, the poet says in the sixth section, will be able to laugh into the face of Death; and in the final section the poet addresses Death directly:

> Pardon, great enemy,
> Without an angry thought
> We've carried in our tree,
> And here and there have bought
> Till all the boughs are gay,
> And she may look from the bed
> On pretty things that may
> Please a fantastic head.
> Give her a little grace,
> What if a laughing eye
> Have looked into your face?
> It is about to die.

UPON A DYING LADY VII

Here the human relevance of art and literature as Yeats conceived of them is being made explicit: their intensity gives a human being a standpoint from which some degree of control over life is possible; through art and literature man can make himself more than the trembling victim of incomprehensible forces such as age and death. But if literature is to have this value, it is clear that it must be more than the mere reflection of human joy or sorrow; it must be a conscious refashioning of experience. This question of whether literature is a direct reflection of life or not is the subject of the dialogue poem, *Ego Dominus Tuus*, where 'hic', the defender of the subjectivity of art, is opposed by 'ille' (or 'Willie' as a contemporary wit put it), who declares that literature should be independent of the artist's personal life, indeed the antithesis of it. Great literature, 'ille' says, is impersonal, reflecting the great poet's desire to hammer out for himself an imaginative, as opposed to his, often unsatisfactory, personal identity:

> By the help of an image
> I call to my own opposite, summon all
> That I have handled least, least looked upon.

In great poetry, poetry which is not 'timid, entangled, empty and abashed' by being merely personal effusions, the poet expresses his 'anti-self', as Dante and Keats did. A poem is the product of powerful personal emotion, but it has an existence, as a work of art, which goes beyond personal emotion. Here Yeats is working his way towards his theory of the poetic 'mask', which is in its turn a reflection of his view, most fully expressed in *A Vision*, his prose exposition of his philosophical system, that within each man subjective and objective, or 'antithetical' and 'primary', impulses are constantly at war, and that decadence results if either is allowed to predominate, in a man, an age, a civilisation or an epoch.

Feeling perhaps that such theories needed some external commentary if he was not to lose his audience, Yeats wrote, in 1918, what he later called 'a text for exposition', *The Phases of the Moon*. To provide an opportunity for the exposition of his 'system', Yeats imagines a quarrel between himself and his creations, Michael Robartes and Owen Aherne. Thus the situation of the poem is that Robartes and Aherne, seeing the poet labouring at his poetry in the tower, mock his efforts to transcend the inescapable cycles of life. Robartes explains to Aherne that life can be described in terms of twenty-eight lunar phases. Roughly speaking, in the first fourteen phases the soul seeks subjective self-fulfilment, particularly after Phase Eight, and in the second fourteen seeks social integration, particularly after Phase Twenty-two: the division between these two movements is the full moon:

> Before the full
> It sought itself and afterwards the world.

Although the fifteenth phase, in its balance of the subjective and objective forces, gives a hint of possible perfection, this balance cannot be maintained, Robartes says, and so the poet is wasting his time in his efforts to create some kind of permanent beauty. Inevitably, this is not, for the most part, a good poem, but it is a very lucid exposition of Yeats's 'system' in outline, and it is saved from mediocrity by the conclusion, when the power of the poet is dramatically demonstrated. These creatures were created by the poet, and they are visible only by the light from the tower window. At the end of the poem they are dismissed by the poet, as he finishes his labours: 'The light in the tower window was put out.' Read in conjunction with *Ego Dominus Tuus*, this poem is an assertion that through a poetic image of 'anti-self' the poet can achieve a victory over the apparently meaningless cycles of life. In great poetry, the poet achieves, permanently, that balance of personal emotion and artistic control, of the antithetical and primary impulses, that the fifteenth phase of the moon hints at. Thus the exposition of poetic theory, *Ego Dominus Tuus*, and the exposition of his system, *The Phases of the Moon*, complement each other and assert the supreme power and relevance of literature and art.

The kind of poetic image that can help the poet to achieve this stability and equilibrium is presented in the final poem of the volume, *The Double Vision of Michael Robartes* of 1919. It is in many ways a triumphant poem, celebrating the poet's resolution, through the poetic image of the dancer, of the conflict between intellect, as represented by the sphinx, and heart, as represented by the buddha. Explaining this poem in *A Vision*, Yeats says these figures represent, respectively: 'the mind's self-begotten unity, an intellectual excitement', and 'the outward-looking mind, love and its lure'. Going on, he says: 'They stand, so to speak, like heraldic supporters guarding the mystery of the fifteenth phase.' At the start of the poem, Robartes is torn by these conflicting forces, but the dancer, symbolising a fusion of intellect and heart, spirit and body, gives a glimpse of the unity of being of the fifteenth phase which mitigates his agony:

> O little did they care who danced between,
> And little she by whom her dance was seen
> So she had outdanced thought.
> Body perfection brought,
>
> For what but eye and ear silence the mind
> With the minute particulars of mankind?
> Mind moved yet seemed to stop
> As 'twere a spinning-top.

The opposites are here resolved into a unified activity, where each receives it due, without being allowed to predominate over the other. After seeing this vision, Robartes no longer feels the helpless pawn of unknown forces ('When had I my own will?') but is elated by this poetic reconciliation of 'the commonness of thought and images/That have the frenzy of our western seas'. This poem is Robartes's 'arrangement' of his vision into a 'song' of gratitude; the sceptical Robartes is now finally converted by the poet. Once again, then, a volume of Yeats's poetry ends on a note of optimism and assurance; the questions are answered, and the conflicts resolved, for the moment at least.

In the course of this volume Yeats can be seen progressing from a fear of age and death and a pervasive feeling of inadequacy and helplessness, to a sense of the irrelevance of age and death and a conviction of the power of his poetic art. Of course, there is no complacency about these attitudes, for the poet recognises the tendency to accept life negatively, to submit to the cycles of existence, and also sees the immense difficulty of achieving a reconciliation of the warring forces within the human personality. As always, however, Yeats pins his faith on the actuality of ordinary life. Thus the 'minute particulars' of human life (a phrase from Blake) prevent the predominance of abstractions or theories. What this volume shows is that the poet's struggle for meaning is no different from the ordinary person's struggle for identity, so that the relevance of literature becomes very obvious. The greatness of this volume is that it presents the doubts and obstacles of the struggle without negative pessimism, and the ultimate triumph without arrogance or complacency.

The continuity of thought between *The Wild Swans at Coole* and *Michael Robartes and the Dancer* (1921) is indicated very clearly by the title of the later volume. In the title poem, Yeats touches upon the possibility that even the dancer may be contaminated by abstract intellectualism. In this poem the dancer's symbolic qualities are more specifically described as feminine qualities, women being more capable than men of uniting mind and body:

> ... all beautiful women may
> Live in uncomposite blessedness,
> And lead us to the like—if they
> Will banish every thought, unless
> The lineaments that please their view
> When the long looking-glass is full,
> Even from the foot-sole think it too.

The poem is a dialogue between Robartes and the dancer, and the dancer is not entirely convinced at the end of the poem that Robartes's views on women are valid: 'They say such different things at school.' This first poem, then, is one of threat to the qualities through which Yeats had achieved confidence and balance in the previous volume. This volume, however, goes on to show how beautiful women may lead men to new levels of intensity and insight through sexual union, and *Solomon and Sheba* and *An Image from a Past life* record such moments of sexual intensity and their significance.

The fine poem, *Under Saturn*, being addressed to his wife, continues this theme of female wisdom while also pointing in new directions. Explaining his saturnine mood to his wife, the poet says that it is caused not by sad memories of lost love and youth, but by his sense of having betrayed an early vow to serve, in some way, his native region of Sligo, and, implicitly, Ireland. This poem, with its Nationalist hints, which was written in November 1918, prepares the reader for the explicitly political poem, *Easter 1916*, written between May and September 1916, but first generally published here. The note of self-criticism which prevails in *Under Saturn* is again conspicuous in this poem, for he begins by saying that he has been guilty of complacent detachment (the kind recorded in *September 1913*) in his attitude towards himself and his fellow-Irishmen: 'Being certain that they and I/But lived where motley is worn.' Now he recognises that through the events of Easter Week his fellow-countrymen have achieved a heroic intensity such as he admires most; they have stopped 'burning damp faggots' and have achieved a permanence which he recognises and confirms by including them in his 'song'. Qualities which he had previously thought the prerogative of people like Robert Gregory have shown themselves among those whom he had derided. Heroic intensity has transcended the cycles of ordinary life, and achieved permanence in the midst of flux:

> Hearts with one purpose alone
> Through summer and winter seem
> Enchanted to a stone
> To trouble the living stream.

EASTER 1916

After recognising the heroism of Easter Week, Yeats ventures to wonder if perhaps their sacrifice was unnecessary: 'For England may keep faith/For all that is done and said.' In spite of these misgivings, however, Yeats ends by granting the men of Easter Week the dignity and immortality of verse, even MacBride:

> And what if excess of love
> Bewildered them till they died?
> I write it out in a verse—
> MacDonagh and MacBride
> And Connolly and Pearse
> Now and in time to be,
> Wherever green is worn,
> Are changed, changed utterly:
> A terrible beauty is born.

'What if it *is* true that they were misguided?' Yeats asks. That does not detract in any way from their achievement; they threw off the motley and achieved tragic stature. Some commentators have suggested that this poem is marred by an element of political prudence; that Yeats expressed misgivings because, uncertain about the ultimate political outcome, he was anxious not to antagonise either side. It is less cynical to see the doubts of the poem as being characteristically Yeatsian; he is, in a sense, the poet of mixed feelings. Why should we expect him to be certain about politics? Indeed, without this uncertainty, the poem would lose a great deal of its tension and complexity which make it one of the finest political poems in the language, as fine, for example, as Marvell's *Horatian Ode* and somewhat similar in its mixed feelings.

Indeed, the poet's mixed feelings about Easter Week are expressed much more resoundingly in a poem, *On a Political Prisoner*, about a woman he admires, Countess Markiewicz, formerly Constance Gore-Booth of Lissadell, Sligo, who suffered imprisonment because of her part in Easter Week. It contrasts her imprisonment with her former freedom, and asserts that she has foolishly sacrificed this freedom for the sake of mere abstract theories. Compared with *Easter 1916*, the poem lacks conviction and complexity; it certainly fails to make its case that her political career is less noble than her former aristocratic pursuits at Lissadell, in spite of the viciousness of the attack on her political enthusiasms: 'Blind and leader of the blind/ Drinking the foul ditch where they lie.' The unsubtle, assertive quality of the poem can perhaps be explained by a comment he made about the poem in a letter: 'I am writing on Con to avoid writing one on Maud. All of them are in prison.' Literally almost, one might say, his heart was not in the poem, as it clearly would have been had he been writing about Maud.

The hatred of abstract fanaticism is the central theme of *The Leaders of the Crowd*, too. More specifically, he says here that the demagogic leaders lack the self-knowledge, produced partly by solitary study, which is necessary in political leaders. The lamp of self-knowledge, 'the student's lamp', is contrasted with the false, misleading light of rhetoric and fanaticism that these leaders hold before the people: 'that lamp is from the tomb.' These views illuminate retrospectively such a poem as *The Scholars*, making it clear that that poem is by no means the naïve attack on study that it is sometimes taken for, and they also look forward to the views he expresses in *Among School Children* on the nature of true wisdom. What makes Yeats particularly suspicious of popular political leaders is their uncomplicated facility, fluency and optimism:

> They must to keep their certainty accuse
> All that are different of a base intent;
> Pull down established honour; hawk for news
> Whatever their loose fantasy invent
> And murmur it with bated breath, as though
> The abounding gutter had been Helicon
> Or calumny a song.

THE LEADERS OF THE CROWD

The contempt of this passage is controlled by a certain play of wit, particularly in the last line and a half, so that this poem has a greater complexity and subtlety than *On a Political Prisoner*. Yeats's pervasive suspicion of facility, of intellectual or emotional short-cuts, is present in his self-analyses as well as in his attitudes to others, as is shown in the poem, *Demon and Beast*, which begins with the calculated ambiguity of 'certain' in the first line:

> For certain minutes at the least
> That crafty demon and that loud beast
> That plague me day and night
> Ran out of my sight.

These few minutes of certainty, of resolution of warring opposites, are cherished by Yeats for the 'aimless joy' they produce in him, but he is at heart suspicious of this certainty, feeling the possibility 'that mere growing old, that brings/Chilled blood, this sweetness brought'. He goes on to say that the sweetness for which he longs is the sweetness of tragic joy rather than of personal happiness, a sweetness which arises from, rather than departs from, life:

68

O what a sweetness strayed
Through barren Thebaid,
Or by the Mareotic sea
When that exultant Antony
And twice a thousand more
Starved upon the shore
And withered to a bag of bones!
What had the Caesars but their thrones?

The men besieged in Thebes, or Antony's soldiers, achieved this tragic joy, and its supreme value is asserted through the arrogant rhetorical question. The emotion being celebrated here is that which led the dying Cleopatra to say: "Tis paltry to be Caesar.'

In *The Second Coming* of January 1919, Yeats again expresses his suspicion of political fanaticism:

The best lack all conviction, while the worst
Are full of passionate intensity.

January 1919 was the month in which the Irish Constituent Assembly, comprising the elected Irish M.P.s from Westminster, met independently, in defiance of England, to declare its Republican sympathies, an act which provoked the formation of an English security force, nicknamed the Black and Tans, which was to be responsible for the 'Terrors' of the next two years. Thus the prophetic, apocalyptic tone of the poem was justified by subsequent events. In the poem Yeats expresses his theories on the rise and fall of civilisation in the terms later propounded in *A Vision*. A civilisation begins with a moment of inspiration or revelation, such as the birth of Christ, and its progress is like the unwinding, or 'perning' to use the dialect word Yeats was fond of, of thread wound on a cone or 'gyre'. Thus, at first a civilisation is very narrow and intense, like the apex of a cone, but it gradually loses its impetus, broadens, and so dissipates its energies. As this happens, an opposite inspiration, which has been gaining strength from an initial state of inactivity and, almost, powerlessness, and which is represented by a cone whose apex is at the centre of the base of the other cone, takes over and begins a new civilisation, one inspired by an antithetically different force from the civilisation it is succeeding. In *A Vision* this constant pattern of movement and counter-movement—reminiscent of Arnold Toynbee's view of history—is represented diagrammatically by Yeats:

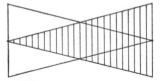

He comments on this diagram:

> If I call the unshaded cone 'Discord' and the other 'Concord' and think of each as the bound of a gyre, I see that the gyre of 'Concord' diminishes as that of 'Discord' increases, and can imagine after that the gyre of 'Concord' increasing while that of 'Discord' diminishes, and so on, one gyre within the other always. Here the thought of Heraclitus dominates all: 'Dying each other's life, living each other's death.' A VISION, p. 68

These are what Yeats calls elsewhere the dry astrological bones of the poem but, though adding a dimension of meaning to the poem, they are by no means indispensable to its understanding. Surveying the contemporary anarchy in Ireland, and indeed throughout Europe, Yeats feels that the forces of Christian love are almost spent, and that a new, more brutal, force is about to take over:

> And what rough beast, its hour come round at last,
> Slouches towards Bethlehem to be born.
>
> THE SECOND COMING

The terrifying cosmic nature of this vision of impending brutality is, in itself, a justification of Yeats's efforts in writing *A Vision*, as is the superb opening image in which the diminishing impetus of Christianity is conveyed through the idea that Christianity is like a falcon that has lost touch with the falconer, and is thus lost and directionless:

> Turning and turning in the widening gyre,
> The falcon cannot hear the falconer.

aspects of his own and his society's situation which most urgently concerned him. Though he is tempted to despair as a result of his acute sense of the difficulties of life, he never succumbs to these temptations. The 'minute particulars' of ordinary life are never sacrificed to a theory, his own or anyone else's, so that there is no clear line of theoretical advance, but rather an increasing wisdom and humanity:

> And wisdom is a butterfly
> And not a gloomy bird of prey.

TOM O'ROUGHLEY

4

'The Tower': 1921–1928

Yeats's purchase of the Norman tower he named 'Thoor Ballylee', situated at Gort, near Coole Park, for the bargain price of £35 in 1917, marks the beginning of new preoccupations, touched upon in *Michael Robartes and the Dancer*, but fully explored in the poems of *The Tower* of 1928. As early as 1900, writing of Shelley's use of the tower symbol, Yeats had seen the tower as a universal symbol of 'a mind looking inward upon itself' and, of course, he was aware of the vogue the symbol was enjoying at that time in such works as *Axel*.

It is typical of Yeats that he should want to own a symbol, as it were; it indicates the strong sense of reality which underlies and strengthens his symbolic methods, 'mythology rooted in the earth', as he put it. Quite apart from its symbolic significance, however, the ownership of the tower made Yeats 'officially' part of the land-owning Anglo-Irish Protestant minority, an allegiance he had felt in the twenty years since his first meeting with Lady Gregory, and which he clung to during the Civil War when this section of the community was the particular target of the Republican forces, in their resistance against the 1921 settlement. Symbolism and realism, metaphysical speculations and contemporary social comment, again jostle each other in the poems of *The Tower*. Although his mind was 'looking inward upon itself', Yeats always wanted to test the findings of his introspection against reality. The poems collected here cover again a long period, from *Owen Aherne and his Dancers* of October 1917 to *Colonus' Praise* of March 1927, and again they are arranged architecturally, each poem contributing to Yeats's continuing argument with himself and to the development of the book, from the uncertainties of *Sailing to Byzantium* to the almost arrogant confidence and assurance of *All Souls' Night*. Like all his collections, this one reveals both continuity and innovation in themes and style. The themes reflect both his own life in this period, and certain perennial concerns which never left him; his style shows his continuing search for a distinctive poetic voice.

The most important aspect of his life during this period was that he became a 'public man', being an active and controversial senator of the Irish Free State from 1922 to 1928. In the Senate he formed another important and revealing friendship, that with the authoritarian and much-hated Kevin O'Higgins, whose assassination in July 1927 distressed and embittered Yeats. In this period, generally, he inclined towards authoritarian forms and methods of government in the belief that only harsh measures could fend off impending anarchy, and he was even attracted to Mussolini's Fascism. Within this same period, he received, in 1923, the Nobel Prize for literature, an honour he relished immensely. And yet, concurrently with this public activity, he was pursuing even more vigorously the intricacies of his 'system'. Thus he devoted the major part of his energies in 1924 to the completion of *A Vision*, which was first published in 1925. In its completed form, *A Vision* represents Yeats's efforts to see human history in terms of a constant battle between two fundamental human impulses, that towards individuality and self-expression and that towards integration and the subordination of self to society. This battle is represented in *A Vision* by the gyres, a more graphic way of expressing the conflict than the lunar circle of, for example, *The Phases of the Moon*. In *A Vision*, he speaks of his system as a 'stylistic arrangement of experience', a phrase which shows that he did not attribute to it a literal or objective truth, but rather saw it as a personal device for staving off a sense of being adrift in time.

It is precisely this combination of public activity with his heightened metaphysical speculations that gives *Among School Children* its exciting contrasts and modulations from the particular to the general, the contemporary to the timeless. In his emotional life, in spite of the happiness of his own marriage, the marriage of Iseult to a man he thought 'a dunce', Francis Stuart, made him feel once again the unpredictability of women's emotions and the physical deprivations of age. Indeed, his health was very uncertain in this period, particularly between 1924 and 1928 when on at least one occasion he was close to death. For health reasons he spent quite lengthy periods in Italy, particularly at Rapallo where Pound was frequently at his side. Public life, ill-health and proximity to death, emotional bitterness, marital happiness, metaphysical speculation: all these elements contributed to the controlled richness of *The Tower*. But underlying all these elements are the complexities and perplexities which Yeats encountered in his exploration of the relation between the world of Imagination and the real world. The question which Keats asked in his *Ode to a Nightingale* about the Imagination, 'Was it a vision or a waking dream?' was one that continued to exercise Yeats's mental and emotional powers in this period. Does the Imagination offer access to a higher plane of reality or merely an escape from reality? Is a reconciliation of Imagination and Reality possible? It is hardly surprising, in view of the diversity and difficulty of these concerns and preoccupations, that this is a demanding collection of poems.

Perhaps this is the first volume in which Yeats achieves consistently a distinctive style, a style capable of ranging from hieratic loftiness to colloquial directness without any sense of strain or incongruity. Certainly Yeats felt that it was the best book he had written, although, as he says in a letter, it astonished him by its bitterness. Perhaps he was determined to make the public see him at last as he was, to banish finally the public image of him as an Irish Romantic poet of the Celtic Twilight. One would guess that he was irritated, as well as amused, by the fact that his *Poems* of 1895 was selling better than ever in this period. Admittedly he had revised some of the early poems included in that volume, out of all recognition, but he still felt that his later work was incomparably superior, less 'dream-burdened' than his earlier poems.

The Tower opens with *Sailing to Byzantium*, a poem which reflects the interest in Byzantine art felt by Yeats since his visit to Ravenna, a city whose churches contain the finest of all Byzantine mosaics, with Lady Gregory and her son in 1907. In the Twenties he deepened and intensified his knowledge by reading several of the books available on Byzantine art and civilisation, which were increasingly fashionable. This interest and reading were part of his search for what he now called 'unity of being', a state in which art and life interpenetrated each other, and which he thought he saw in Byzantine culture. The height of Byzantine culture occurs in the Fifteenth Phase, and in *A Vision* Yeats describes his Byzantium in a famous passage:

> I think if I could be given a month of Antiquity and leave to spend it where I chose, I would spend it in Byzantium. . . . I think that in early Byzantium, maybe never before or since in recorded history, religious, aesthetic and practical life were one, that architect and artificers . . . spoke to the multitude and the few alike. The painter, the mosaic worker, the worker in gold and silver, the illuminator of sacred books, were almost impersonal, almost perhaps without the consciousness of individual design, absorbed in their subject-matter and that the vision of a whole people. A VISION, pp. 279–80

This passage is notable for its certainty and assurance, but these qualities evaporate in the poem itself, in which Yeats finds himself torn between extremities, obliged to make a choice. The poem is the personal drama of that attempted choice, as embodied within an ageing poet. Rejected by the cruel world of birth, generation and death as obsolete, the poet determines to sail to a place where he will be appreciated, Byzantium. He hopes that he will thus be able to defeat Time, 'spit into the face of Time' (to quote his contemporary revision of *The Lamentation of the Old Pensioner*), because art is timeless. He wants to sail from the 'sensual music' made by the birds—'that dying generation'—to the ethereal music made by the Byzantine birds of 'hammered gold and gold enamelling'. And yet, in spite of the fervour of his resolution, and the good reasons for it, this is a poem of regret, uncertainty and the rootlessness that follows rejection. Seen at close quarters, Byzantium is less attractive than at a distance, in rather the same way that Keats's nightingale becomes a deceiver after examination. Thus, to compare the first stanza with its 'richly concrete evocation of instinctive life' (to quote Professor Knights) with the last stanza, in which art, in the form of a golden bird, serves merely to 'kill time' for the lords and ladies of Byzantium, is to sense a deliberate drop in vitality. 'Killing time' is fine for those who like their time dead, but Yeats was not such a man, and so one feels in this final stanza an emotional revulsion away from the passivity of the state which had seemed so desirable in theory. Implicitly, Yeats the poet feels that art should be able to speak to the world of the first stanza if it is not to be trivial and sterile. In Byzantium timelessness is achieved at too great a cost. For example, in the last stanza, the repetition 'gold and gold' suggests the limitations of this world, as does the passivity of 'set', whereas the linguistic inventiveness and rhythmic vitality of the first stanza reveal the speaker's deepest allegiances:

> The salmon-falls, the mackerel-crowded seas,
> Fish, flesh, or fowl, commend all summer long
> Whatever is begotten, born, and dies.
> Caught in that sensual music all neglect
> Monuments of unageing intellect.

SAILING TO BYZANTIUM

The declared allegiance to art and its 'monuments of unageing intellect' rings hollow after the previous lines. 'Mackerel-crowded', with its compression of sounds, suggests an overflowing fecundity, and the departure from the rhythmic norm in 'fish, flesh, or fowl' suggests an attraction felt by the speaker in spite of himself. The timelessness of art is no compensation for the loss of such fullness; any more than is the 'cold pastoral' art of Keats's Grecian Urn. The eternity of Byzantium is an artifice: it is artificial in a pejorative as well as in a literal sense. If this is all the 'singing-masters' of his soul, the Byzantine mosaic sages, can teach him, the problems caused by *that* country's neglect and rejection remain unsolved. What makes this a great poem is its supreme honesty; both the world of the young and the world of Byzantium are presented honestly; they are both beautiful, but the poet's allegiance to the world of generation goes too deep to be rooted out, however much he might want to.

After the uncertainties of *Sailing to Byzantium*, the poem *The Tower* explores the possibilities of a different kind of poetic Imagination and as a result achieves some measure of confidence. The poet begins by facing up to the suggestion that with old age he should turn aside from the more intense aspects of life and 'be content with argument and deal/In abstract things': things like the idealistic philosophies of Plato and Plotinus. Here Plotinus, a neo-Platonist of the third century, is linked with Plato as being out of touch with human life, but when *The Tower* appeared Yeats added a note retracting his statement about both of them, saying that he was wrong to 'see them as all transcendence'. From about 1925 onwards, Plotinus, in Stephen MacKenna's translation, became one of his favourite philosophers, as is shown in, for example, *The Delphic Oracle upon Plotinus*. Yeats, however, after *Sailing to Byzantium*, knows something of the dangers of the esoteric uses of the Imagination, and so, in the second section of the poem, he brings to life through his poetic powers not golden Byzantine sages but figures from local Ballylee legend. These are his new singing-masters and he calls them to life, as he had the sages, to 'ask a question of them all'. These figures (described at unnecessary length by Yeats in a note on the poem) teach him, through the glimpse his imagination affords him of their vitality, the folly of 'turning aside' from life, however old one might be, a point reinforced by the implicit counsel of his own poetic creation, Red Hanrahan, who shows him at the end of the second section the folly of being guided by such abstractions as pride, cowardice or conscience. Whereas in the previous poem, the sages, admittedly at his own request, had led his imagination away from life, here the blind poet Raftery and the rest lead him back to life so that, reconciled to life, he can declare his faith in man, and 'mock Plotinus' thought/And cry in Plato's teeth'. What he cries is that man is at the centre of the world, not abstractions. Thus, in the poem as a whole he accepts life, as seen from the vantage point of the tower battlements, and declares his faith that, provided the

Imagination retains its vital contact with ordinary human experience, the conventional consequence of old age, retreat into abstractions from actual life, need not apply to the poet.

These two fine poems can be seen, therefore, as part of the continuing Yeatsian dialectic about the relation between the world of Imagination and the real world, a problem which became more acute as, with old age impending, the satisfactions of the real world became less obviously realisable to Yeats the man. In a sense, Yeats the poet is resisting the temptations now felt increasingly by Yeats the man. The basic question behind these two poems is this: Is the poetic imagination of an ageing man better employed in helping him to escape the ingratitude and indignities of the real world, by creating for him a timeless, aesthetic world, or in helping him to make sense of the real world? At the end of the poem *The Tower* Yeats has fended off the aesthetic temptations, but temptation will come in this kind again.

The long poem, *Meditations in Time of Civil War* of 1921-2, is based on Yeats's own experiences at Thoor Ballylee during the fighting between the Republicans and the Free Staters which broke out in the summer of 1921. Although in a sense a political poem, therefore, its political content is subordinate to Yeats's exploration of the nature of the poet's role in violent times, and there is no trace here of the harshly repressive attitude to the Republicans which he felt as a man. The poem begins with a statement of the, for Yeats, frightening possibility that all the social values cherished by him are, in these anarchic times, obsolete and irrelevant. Thus, he says, buildings which once symbolised a noble, heroic way of life are insignificant if 'the great-grandson of that house,/For all its bronze and marble, 's but a mouse'; lines which are, in their realistic honesty, sufficient refutation of those who accuse Yeats of an unthinking allegiance to an idealised past. He goes on to say that if this is the case, if a former way of life which had inspired poets like him is indeed outmoded, then he can have no other function than to express poetically 'befitting emblems of adversity'. Then, however, an alternative to this peripheral poetic activity suggests itself to him as he reflects on the significance of a medieval Japanese sword, given him by a friend, Juazo Sato. Such a work of art, produced by an 'aching heart', is more than an emblem of adversity. In Sato's sword, art has produced something permanent *and* combative, something more positive than an emblem of adversity and more, one might say, sharply relevant to the world. Sato's sword, one of Yeats's most cherished possessions, encourages him at this moment of doubt, but when he actually meets, on the road at his door, the soldiers of the Civil War, he again feels envy, feels that he is a mere dreamer compared with these men of action. These misgivings are beautifully expressed in Section VI of the poem, *The Stare's Nest by my Window*. In the first stanza he expresses his sense of the disintegration of his personal values, and the need for reconstruction:

> The bees build in the crevices
> Of loosening masonry, and there
> The mother birds bring grubs and flies.
> My wall is loosening; honey-bees,
> Come build in the empty house of the stare.

'My wall is loosening' is particularly moving in its quiet intensity. Just as the starlings (stares) and bees are building in this loosening masonry, so the poet must rebuild his imagination, basing the reconstruction on love rather than fantasy:

> We had fed the heart on fantasies,
> The heart's grown brutal from the fare;
> More substance in our enmities
> Than in our love; O honey-bees,
> Come build in the empty house of the stare.

Here again the self-criticism is profound and provides the impetus for imaginative reconstruction. In the final section of the poem, Yeats starkly juxtaposes the achievements of his poetic imagination, 'self-delighting reverie', and the realities of contemporary Ireland, 'grip of claw and the eye's complacency', wondering if perhaps a life of action would have been more satisfying than the poetic life, but in the end decides that even the tantalisingly partial insights of poetry are preferable to the 'noisy complacency' of politicians: 'The innumerable clanging wings that have put out the moon.' It would be wrong, however, to say that this poem ends confidently, for the word 'abstract' is always critical in Yeats, and 'suffice' is an equivocal word.

> The abstract joy,
> The half-read wisdom of daemonic images,
> Suffice the ageing man as once the growing boy.

There can be no doubt that this period of Civil War was a period of deep depression for Yeats, through which he was sustained by his belief in his ability to remake himself and his imagination, but this was to be a long process, and he never regained the kind of confidence he had derived in the previous decade from Coole Park. The writing of *A Vision* was, as he put it in a letter of 1937, 'a last act of defence against the chaos of the world', but after the Civil War his imagination was increasingly cataclysmic.

Nineteen Hundred and Nineteen, written between 1919 and 1922 and originally called *Thoughts upon the Present State of the World*, is another poem of profound and scathing self-criticism and re-orientation. Thus, surveying the evidence for the universality of the destructive impulse in all ages and civilisations, he looks back to the optimistic beliefs he had shared with Lady Gregory and others and makes a cruelly unfair indictment of them:

> We too had many pretty toys when young:
> A law indifferent to blame or praise,
> To bribe or threat; habits that made old wrong
> Melt down, as it were wax in the sun's rays;
> Public opinion ripening for so long
> We thought it would outlive all future days.
> O what fine thought we had because we thought
> That the worst rogues and rascals had died out.

And yet, the poem goes on, man cannot escape from such naïve and vulnerable idealism:

> But is there any comfort to be found?
> Man is in love and loves what vanishes,
> What more is there to say?

The central emotions of the poem are beautifully presented through the symbolic comparison of the soul to a swan, at once beautiful and pathetic:

> The wings half spread for flight,
> The breast thrust out in pride
> Whether to play, or to ride
> Those winds that clamour of approaching night.

Thinking of how 'crack-pated' his early ideals now seem, he is tempted to despair, and yet, like the swan, those ideals had a kind of fragile beauty. Nothing is more typical of Yeats's mature style, nor more revealing of his emotional integrity and strength, than the juxtaposition of the beauty and mystery of the swan symbol with the contemptuous colloquialism, 'crack-pated'. The tone of self-mockery is prominent throughout the poem, but there is a dramatic change of direction as Yeats turns on the cynics, the mockers, who are incapable of cherishing any ideals, and says that they equally deserve and receive mockery: 'for we/Traffic in mockery.' In this magnificent Section V of the poem Yeats is rhetorical in the best sense of that word, achieving a sustained eloquence of indignation quite as fine as Blake's rather similar poem, 'Mock on, mock on, Voltaire, Rousseau!' The poem ends with a vision of evil gathering force as he presents a wild procession of witches, which concludes with a symbol of universal depravity, the tributes, 'bronzed peacock-feathers, red combs of her cocks', offered by a witch to her incubus; his age, Yeats implies, offers similar tributes to the forces of chaos and evil. Is there, then, any comfort to be found? Only the comfort of a knowledge of the universality of destructive forces, which brings with it a conviction that even naïve idealism is preferable to mocking cynicism. As in *Meditations in Time of Civil War*, Yeats finds some comfort, but it is partial and equivocal.

In *Meditations in Time of Civil War*, Yeats's political views are subsumed into the historical perspectives presented in *A Vision*, and this process is even more marked in *Leda and the Swan*, where Yeats presents his historical philosophy with immense dramatic force. Yeats tells us in a note on the poem that it began as a political poem, written at the request of an editor of a political publication, and his summary of his original political intention makes it seem likely that it would have been Fascist in tone. He begins by saying that the 'individualist, demagogic movement' is 'exhausted', and goes on:

> Then I thought: 'Nothing is now possible but some movement from above preceded by some violent annunciation.' My fancy began to play with Leda and the Swan for metaphor and I began this poem; but as I wrote, bird and lady took such possession of the scene that all politics went out of it.   VARIORUM EDITION, p. 828

Metaphor takes over from personal opinion, so that the finished poem—over which Yeats took immense pains—retains no trace of the original political intention. It presents what Yeats saw as the moment of birth of Greek civilisation—the rape of Leda by Zeus, in the form of a swan, an event at once horrifying and awe-inspiring—as symbolic of the subsequent course of that civilisation:

> A shudder in the loins engenders there
> The broken wall, the burning roof and tower
> And Agamemnon dead.
>
> LEDA AND THE SWAN

The poem's syntax, with the deliberate suspension of a finite verb in the first section and the almost total absence of any time reference, suggests the meaning. Man's subjection to time can be mitigated by an awareness of the essential similarity, almost simultaneity, of all time: here in one intense moment of 'annunciation' is the whole course of Greek civilisation, and every civilisation begins with a similarly violent annunciation before following an opposite course to the civilisation it is superseding. As he writes in *A Vision*: 'Each age unwinds the thread another age had wound.' The accomplishment of the writing in *Leda and the Swan* expresses the confidence which this view of history gave Yeats. Through such insights he could 'break the teeth of Time' (*The New Faces*).

Approximately at the centre of the volume *The Tower* is an oblique poetic manifesto, *On a Picture of a Black Centaur by Edmund Dulac*. The central distinction made by the poem, however, relates to this volume's preoccupation with time: the distinction between a kind of poetry that is soon swallowed up by time and a kind that survives. As he looks at the picture of a mythological creature, a black centaur, this creature comes to represent for him the treacherous attractions of a mythological poetry, the kind of poetry he now dismisses as 'horse-play'. Such poetry is soon, deservedly, swallowed up by time, but now, he says, he is dealing with universal and eternal themes which defy time:

> . . . but now
> I bring full-flavoured wine out of a barrel found
> Where seven Ephesian topers slept and never knew
> When Alexander's empire passed, they slept so sound.

Although he has escaped the clutches of the kind of poetry symbolised by the centaur, Yeats admits that he must remain awake to the dangers if he is not to succumb to the beauty of 'those horrible green birds', and so he tells the centaur to sleep now that its age, like Saturn's, is over, while he remains watchfully awake: 'I have loved you better than my soul for all my words.' This note of lingering fondness for an area of experience which is being rejected gives the poem a subtlety and complexity not often found in poems of rejection. The poem, then, is a resolution to draw poetic inspiration from less recondite sources, to stop gathering 'old mummy wheat/In the mad abstract dark' because of his new realisation that 'what wholesome sun has ripened is wholesome food to eat,/And that alone'. How seriously he took this resolution of 1920 is shown in most of his subsequent poems, where he is at constant pains to achieve lucidity and make his experience accessible to the reader. He was fond, in later years, of quoting Goethe's dictum that every poet must have a philosophy but that it must never show in his poetry. Indeed the poem that follows directly on the black centaur poem, *Among School Children*, shows him taking as the starting point an everyday occasion in his life as a senator.

During his term as senator Yeats was a member of a government committee commissioned to investigate the state of Irish education, and this poem, of June 1926, is based on a visit he paid to a school with a reputation for modern and enlightened methods—St. Otteran's, Waterford, which used the Montessori method with its four- to seven-year-olds and placed a similar emphasis on spontaneity and self-expression throughout the school. Yeats's was a genuine interest in education, and he was familiar with the Montessori methods, and with other contemporary educational theories, in particular those presented by an Italian educationist, Gentile, in his book *The Reformation of Education*, with their central emphasis on education as 'a becoming of the spirit', with soul and body being cultivated equally and concurrently. Though the poem as a whole is, as he calls it in a letter, a 'curse upon old age', the educational content is essential to its meaning. In the first stanza, youth, as represented by the children, and age, represented by 'a kind old nun', a teacher, and Yeats himself, 'a sixty-year-old smiling public man', are juxtaposed, with words like 'histories', 'modern' and 'momentary' emphasising the passing of time (Yeats himself quite possibly figured in their History and English lessons). The poet is impressed by the educational methods he observes and the balance they strike between intellectual, practical, aesthetic and spiritual elements, so that there is no trace of irony in the phrase 'the best modern way'. It is important for his later expression of reservations about education as a whole that the education observed in this opening stanza should be accepted as the best. The second stanza introduces an allusion, whose implications are developed later, to Leda, the mother of Helen, and also recalls how Maud and he had, in the distant past, been as one in their shared antipathy to memories of school: 'it seemed that our two natures blent/Into a sphere.' The word 'seemed' is ominous, however, and the reader knows about the subsequent course of their relationship. Will these children, even with their enlightened education, fare any better in life? In the third stanza, his strong personal emotion breaks through his official composure as he thinks he sees something of Maud's past beauty in the children before him, but this illusion is shattered by his recollection of how Maud looks now: still beautiful, certainly, but gauntly so, like a painting of a woman by an early Renaissance Italian painter. He then tries to see himself with similar objectivity, and manages to accept his own gaunt image:

> Better to smile on all that smile, and show
> There is a comfortable kind of old scarecrow.

AMONG SCHOOL CHILDREN

The controlled irony of this was achieved by Yeats only after immense difficulty with these and the preceding lines. (In the poem's first printed version, in *The Dial* in August 1927, he says in the preceding lines that he has wrongs enough to brood over, a note of self-pity which would have destroyed the tone of firm self-control if it had persisted.) Having regained his public composure, through this self-depreciatory irony, he explores in stanzas five and six the ravages of time: a baby's 'shape' soon becomes, after a brief period of beauty, an old man's shape, and, stanza six asserts, intellectual beauty and power fare no better. Thus mothers and lovers are tortured and mocked by images of mortal, transient beauty. The 'kind old nun' by his side reminds him of a different kind of image, and of the love felt by those who dedicate themselves to religion, but, he says, these people are no less cruelly tortured, though very differently. Whereas human images torture mothers and lovers through their transience and changes, these religious images, which 'keep a marble or a bronze repose', also 'break hearts', because of their coldness and lack of change. Human love and religious love are both mocked by these images or 'presences', though the kinds of mockery are antithetically different. At this point, therefore, the poem is poised on the cruel paradox that both change and lack of change mock and torment mankind. This is, approximately, the unresolved paradox of *Sailing to Byzantium*. In *Among School Children*, however, Yeats attempts to resolve this paradox by presenting images which are more inclusive than the images of the first seven stanzas. The final stanza begins with a magnificent ambiguity:

> Labour is blossoming or dancing where
> The body is not bruised to pleasure soul,
> Nor beauty born out of its own despair,
> Nor blear-eyed wisdom out of midnight oil.

'Labour' means both work and the pangs of birth. These, the poet says, become meaningful when the opposites which have tormented the poet himself and the poem's characters are fused into an organic unity. Body/soul, emotion/intellect, these antitheses can be resolved, and in two magnificently daring questions Yeats shows how:

> O chestnut-tree, great-rooted blossomer,
> Are you the leaf, the blossom or the bole?
> O body swayed to music, O brightening glance,
> How can we know the dancer from the dance?

They are self-mocking questions, being ultimately fatuous. There is no way of distinguishing the leaf, the blossom and the bole (trunk) from their identities as parts of a tree, nor of distinguishing between the physical movements of the dancer and the aesthetic aspects of her performance. In such cases, opposites are resolved, parts synthesised into a total being or activity. It is no longer a case of Either/Or, but rather of Both/And. This is the ultimate wisdom about life, and Yeats has learned it through his mistakes and his suffering. The enlightened education these children are receiving is at least a good start to their search for such wisdom, but wisdom must arise from experience and so education can be no more than a start. Eventually, as with all great poems, the experience which *is* the poem defies further analysis, but one is left with a supremely rich, intense and honest presentation of human aspirations. The poem is truly tragic in that it sees clearly human suffering and waste and yet achieves a glimpse of how they can be transcended.

As Hugh Kenner has pointed out, the 'where' of 'Labour is blossoming or dancing where/The body is not bruised to pleasure soul' is given an emphasis which suggests that the blossoming tree and the dancing girl can be given a specific location. This location, the next poem shows, is the ancient Greek province of Colonus. *Colonus' Praise*, from his version of *Oedipus at Colonus*, is a song of praise about this district because here body and spirit co-exist harmoniously:

> And yonder in the gymnasts' garden thrives
> The self-sown, self-begotten shape that gives
> Athenian intellect its mastery,
> Even the grey-leaved olive-tree
> Miracle-bred out of the living stone.

The miraculous olive-tree is significantly in the gymnasts' garden in this timeless world, which also includes dancers, 'immortal ladies', but the timeless perfection of this world includes a pious respect for its physical origins:

> Because this country has a pious mind
> And so remembers that when all mankind
> But trod the road, or splashed about the shore,
> Poseidon gave it bit and oar,
> Every Colonus lad or lass discourses
> Of that oar and of that bit.

There is no mockery of the body by the spirit here, because neither exists separately, but jointly in a perfect union.

Wisdom and *The Fool by the Roadside* make further contributions to Yeats's efforts to define this almost mystical union of body and spirit. Christ is seen as a unique combination of the human and the divine in the first of these poems, and in the second the fool is a fool precisely because of his despair in life, his other-worldly pessimism.

A great deal of the power and complexity of the poems in *The Tower* derives from the way in which they incorporate skilfully and unobtrusively snippets of autobiography. *Owen Aherne and the Dancers*, in which Aherne speaks for Yeats, is a dialogue between the regretful and nostalgic poet and the triumphant and mocking heart. The poem was actually written in October 1917 but it contributes very aptly to the thematic architecture of *The Tower*. Yeats regrets shirking the challenge offered to him by Iseult years previously (she had proposed to him at the age of fifteen), but the heart is callously unsympathetic and unrepentant about having led him astray. The poet reflects that in spite of his intellectual ability—'I can exchange opinion with any neighbouring mind'—he missed one of the most important opportunities of his life because, instead of co-existing harmoniously, his intellect and his heart were in conflict. As in *Among School Children*, this conflict brings mockery, and the heart ends on a note of exultant sadism: 'O let her choose a young man now and all for his wild sake.' There is no resolution of the conflict here; only a warning about the permanent consequences of allowing the heart to predominate over the intellect.

A Man Young and Old is similarly concerned with the consequences of an imbalance between intellect and emotion. Thus the first two sections accuse Maud of a moon-like aloofness that inhibited Yeats so much that he repressed his feelings and is now agonised by the memories. Section III, *The Mermaid*, expresses with superbly economical irony Maud's stupidly unfeeling attitude towards him:

> A mermaid found a swimming lad,
> Picked him for her own,
> Pressed her body to his body,
> Laughed; and plunging down
> Forgot in cruel happiness
> That even lovers drown.

Perhaps they were both at fault, perhaps Yeats could have changed Maud's attitude, but most of the blame belongs to Maud. In Section V, *The Empty Cup*, the poet is driven wild by the memory of lost opportunities. As he says in a letter of this period: 'One looks back to one's youth as to a cup that a mad man dying of thirst left half-tasted.' And yet there is more than bitterness in this poem, because Yeats recalls that in his youth there were moments of intense pleasure which now help to assuage the contempt generally accorded old age. And, since the insulting processes of time are universal, laughter and gaiety seem a more appropriate response to the situation than bitterness or nostalgia. In fact, he says in Section IX, age has certain compensations provided one can control the eruptions of wildness touched on in Section X. The poem ends by recommending an attitude of dispassionate acceptance of Time's insults, since there is nothing to be gained by protest. This astringently pessimistic poem adds to the volume's complexity for it shows that the kind of wisdom and resolution of opposites touched on in earlier poems is not easily achieved, even by the poet himself:

> Even from that delight memory treasures so,
> Death, despair, division of families, all entanglements of mankind
> grow,
> As that old wandering beggar and these God-hated children know.

This pessimism is reinforced by the political cynicism of *The Three Monuments*. Three former statesmen, now commemorated by monuments and quoted as examples of purity, look down on the contemporary political scene and hear the same old platitudes and exhortations: 'The three old rascals laugh aloud.'

All Souls' Night, too, is concerned with the dead, but these dead are very different from the politicians. Whereas the politicians were exclusively concerned with public life, these friends recalled by Yeats were concerned with the after-life and spiritual reality. After invoking their spirits, he realises belatedly, while meditating on one of the friends who encouraged him in his occult beliefs when he was in his twenties, MacGregor Mathers, that they might not be a sympathetic audience after all, might not be willing to listen to human wisdom or partake of the muscatel fumes their host has kindly provided:

> For meditations upon unknown thought
> Make human intercourse grow less and less;
> They are neither paid nor praised.
> But he'd object to the host,
> The glass because my glass;
> A ghost-lover he was
> And may have grown more arrogant being a ghost.

These lines illustrate the buoyant confidence of the poem. The figures he had called to mind in the poem *The Tower* had been able to teach him something about the life they had relished, but these, he decides, have nothing to teach him. Thus, in the second stanza he had declared his need for an audience for his 'marvellous' truth, but in the final stanza he says: 'I need no other thing.' Since 'the living mock' he has had to turn to spirits, but if they are to listen they will have to be humanised with the help of muscatel fumes. Only then can he tell them the marvellous truth he has discovered, a truth which encompasses the whole of human experience:

> Such thought—such thought have I that hold it tight
> Till meditation master all its parts,
> Nothing can stay my glance
> Until that glance run in the world's despite
> To where the damned have howled away their hearts,
> And where the blessed dance;
> Such thought, that in it bound
> I need no other thing,
> Wound in mind's wandering
> As mummies in the mummy-cloth are wound.

In these lines there is a magnificent balance of excitement, enthusiasm and wit. Thus in the first six lines he is almost unable to contain his excitement, and then in the final four lines of the poem he wittily defines his achievement. He, while still a human being, has achieved truths which eluded their spirituality in life and which are now beyond their experience, since they are dead. Although alive, he is 'wound in mind's wandering/As mummies in the mummy-cloth are wound': he has it both ways, and his excitement is thus understandable. *All Souls' Night* is perhaps the most confident poem Yeats ever wrote. Its probable date, November 1920, reveals the reasons for this confidence; this was the period in which, spurred on by his wife's encouragement and gifts, he was beginning to formulate the ideas later incorporated in *A Vision*. It is true that all his volumes end with a more or less convinced affirmation of optimism, but *A Vision* undoubtedly provided very solid ballast for the storm-tossed mind and emotions of Yeats.

The emotional progress outlined in *The Tower* is dramatic,

but one knows that his struggles are not over. After all, the declaration of confidence, *All Souls' Night*, was written six years before the agonised uncertainties of the first poem in the volume, *Sailing to Byzantium*. Since Yeats's arrangement of his poems was always deliberate, one can assume that he felt confident in 1927 when he chose to end *The Tower* on a note of exaltation, but, as he knew, his mind worked through contraries and vacillations, and any equilibrium or balance of these contraries was momentary. In *The Tower*, the poem which justifies the confidence expressed in *All Souls' Night* and prevents it from seeming arrogant is *Among School Children*. In this poem Yeats expressed his most radical doubts, and resolved them; fused opposites through his imaginative intensity. After it, though there are, of course, still doubts, one senses an underlying assurance. The poem is as central to Yeats's work and development as *King Lear* is to Shakespeare's. Like Shakespeare, after his central exploration of his doubts Yeats turns to an exploration of new sources of life, the wild wisdom of Crazy Jane.

5

Crazy Jane and Ribh: 1927–1935

The Tower sold well and was enthusiastically received by the critics, and this success was welcome to Yeats, for the closing years of the 1920s were on the whole bitter and disappointing ones for him. Indeed the whole period between 1927 and 1935, the year of *A Full Moon in March*, was one of withdrawal from public life, and of illness (and almost death), travel, convalescence, and of closer friendship with Pound at Rapallo. Illness and disappointment concentrated his thoughts, and intensified his ambition to write a poetry of revelatory simplicity. His term as senator ended in the summer of 1928, and the government, which was now increasingly Catholic in its sympathies and acts, did not renew his nomination. This heightened Yeats's natural anti-religious and anti-Catholic feelings, a fact reflected in the Crazy Jane and Ribh poems. A large part of 1929 was spent quietly in Ireland, mainly in Dublin, and he finally sold his tower in the summer of that year, before going to Rapallo for the winter. Of the poems he was writing in 1929, he said: 'They are the opposite of my recent work and all praise of joyous life.' In spite of his public disappointments, his faith in 'man's resinous heart' (a phrase from *Resurrection*, a play of this period) remained firm. Perhaps the most important event of this period was the death of Lady Gregory in 1932, an event which intensified the need he already felt to look for a less vulnerable guide to life than the fixed 'code' of values she represented (the word is from *A Vision*). In spite of his serious illnesses in this period, Yeats's imagination is by no means eschatological; indeed his thirst for life increases. In actual politics, his flirtation with Fascism was renewed, though only briefly, through his enthusiasm for an

Irish Fascist movement led by General O'Duffy. If there is a central symbolic event in this period it is his decision of 1934 to undergo a rejuvenation operation. The 'remaking' of his mind and emotions which had gone on for almost twenty years is now extended to his body and his physical appetites. Certainly he felt a renewed zest for life after the operation, and the *Supernatural Songs* of the summer of 1934 show clearly enough his renewed sexual preoccupation.

Intellectually, Yeats continued to learn from Blake, and other influences which intensified his concern with energy and intensely-expressed life were Swift, Nietzsche and Rabelais. An old favourite, Balzac, was reread during the winter of 1931–2, and in philosophy he developed his knowledge of, and enthusiasm for, Plotinus. All these writers he admired because of their central commitment to life as opposed to abstractions. Probably from his reading of Blake he realised again the possibilities of the ballad form, and he employs it frequently in the poems of this period. His continuing openness to new experiences is indicated by, for example, his enthusiasm for *Lady Chatterley's Lover*, and his hopes for Ireland by the prominent part he played in the newly-formed Irish Academy of Letters.

Words for Music Perhaps, which contains the Crazy Jane poems, was published in 1932 by the Cuala Press, but *The Winding Stair and Other Poems* of 1933 appears first in *Collected Poems* and, as always with Yeats's arrangement of his work, this is the logical order in which to consider the two volumes. *The Winding Stair and Other Poems* marks a transition from the social preoccupations of *The Tower* to the intense, manic vision presented in *Words for Music Perhaps*, having as its primary preoccupations a concern with women, particularly Lady Gregory, and with the Yeatsian aesthetic, so that the tone is personal but has behind it references to society and to Yeats's life and thought which are absent from *Words for Music Perhaps*. All this is put much more succinctly and memorably by Yeats himself when he summarises the spirit of this poetry: 'The swordsman throughout repudiates the saint.' Energy takes precedence over sanctity, action over introspection, or, to quote one of his favourite aphorisms from Blake, 'Everything that lives is holy'.

The title of *The Winding Stair and Other Poems* is probably an allusion to Dante's winding stair ('escalina') which leads from the ordinary, corrupt world to an ideal, celestial world. But Dante was more congenial to Eliot than to Yeats, and the allusion is an ironic one here. The temptation is to climb the winding stair, and leave irksome actualities behind, but Yeats characteristically resists the temptation in favour of ordinary life, even if it can sometimes seem to be merely 'a blind man battering blind men'. For Yeats, it is clear by now, the Imagination is firmly established as a means of celebrating and vindicating human life, not of escaping from it. This attitude shows itself immediately in the first poem of the volume, *In Memory of Eva Gore-Booth and Con Markiewicz*. Here he uses his poetic powers to insult Time, which has insulted these two sisters, once the beautiful daughters of Lissadell, now mere 'shadows'. Their political convictions have achieved nothing permanent, but the poet says he can undo the ravages of Time. Man is at the centre of the universe —'We the great gazebo built'—and the poet proves this by re-creating their former beauty, wresting it from the 'shears' of Time:

> The light of evening, Lissadell,
> Great windows open to the south,
> Two girls in silk kimonos, both
> Beautiful, one a gazelle.

The poem ends on a wild, exultant note as the poet rejoices in his power to burn through Time and its consequences: 'Bid me strike a match and blow.' This is a great poem simply because within it Yeats justifies his claims for poetry by recreating a timeless beauty. What one remembers from the poem is not the unhappiness and gauntness of the old sisters but the beauty and grace of their youth. 'A raving autumn shears/Blossom from the summer's wreath', but Yeats miraculously reverses the process so that the sisters blossom again. The tone of defiance continues in the next poem, *Death*, written on the assassination of Kevin O'Higgins, where man, confronted with death, behaves not like a 'dying animal' but 'casts derision' on death. 'Dying animal', of course, is a deliberate echo of *Sailing to Byzantium*:

Consume my heart away; sick with desire
And fastened to a dying animal
It knows not what it is; and gather me
Into the artifice of eternity.

The allusion shows how much confidence Yeats gained in the
year between the composition of the two poems. *Sailing to
Byzantium* was written in September 1926, and *Death* in September 1927. In *Death* man's heart has the confidence to assert its
own value, whereas in *Sailing to Byzantium* it is lost and bewildered, casting around desperately for a refuge.

Characteristically, the next poem, *A Dialogue of Self and Soul*,
introduces a divergent viewpoint, that of spiritual disdain for
human life as expressed by 'My soul', but only to refute it. His
soul calls Yeats up the winding stair, towards Heaven and away
from life. Here, the soul promises, all contradictions and perplexities are resolved: 'intellect no longer knows/*Is* from the
Ought, or *Knower* from the *Known*.' The reply of 'My Self' to
this temptation shows in its every nuance the positive values
that underlie Yeats's later poetry:

I am content to follow to its source
Every event in action or in thought;
Measure the lot; forgive myself the lot!
When such as I cast out remorse
So great a sweetness flows into the breast
We must laugh and we must sing,
We are blest by everything,
Everything we look upon is blest.

The central temptation resisted here is one that becomes particularly attractive with old age, the temptation to recant the beliefs
and emotions of one's youth and fix one's eyes on spiritual
things. Yeats will have nothing to do with such hypocrisy and
simulated 'remorse'. Instead, looking back over his life, he, with
magnificent arrogance, forgives *himself*. The soul's attitude,
summarised in the phrase, 'the crime of death and birth', is
rejected resoundingly. It is a phrase which reminds one of, for
example, *Waiting for Godot*, and there is little doubt that Yeats
would have found much of contemporary pessimism sterile.

The same antithesis between the spiritual and the physically emotional is presented symbolically in *Blood and the Moon*, and Yeats expresses a similar distaste for the cold aloofness symbolised by the moon, and re-affirms an allegiance to life:

> For wisdom is the property of the dead,
> A something incompatible with life; and power,
> Like everything that has the stain of blood,
> A property of the living.

The poet must assert the creative power of the human Imagination, not capitulate to pessimism or despair, Yeats constantly implies, and in the magnificently sardonic *Three Movements* he writes his own version of literary history, seeing an ever-increasing failure of nerve and imaginative strength:

> Shakespearian fish swam the sea, far away from land;
> Romantic fish swam in nets coming to the hand;
> What are all those fish that lie gasping on the strand?

A similar point is made symbolically in *The Crazed Moon*. He sees contemporary poetry as being escapist, concerned only with sources of inspiration long since exhausted, and therefore dying of inanition. The gist of this is expressed in the supremely daring and original opening image:

> Crazed through much child-bearing
> The moon is staggering in the sky.

The traditional symbol of purity has never been more effectively stood on its head. The third stanza of the poem is reminiscent of *The Stare's Nest by my Window*, where Yeats said that his generation's heart grew brutal from the exclusive fare of fantasy:

> Fly-catchers of the moon,
> Our hands are blenched, our fingers seem
> But slender needles of bone;
> Blenched by that malicious dream
> They are spread wide that each
> May rend what comes in reach.

This, then, is another of Yeats's magnificent poetic manifestos which show how perceptive a critic he was of his own and others' work.

Perhaps the centre of this book, certainly its most explicit and positive statement of Yeats's artistic and human values, is *Coole Park, 1929*. The mood of the poem reflects the fact that Lady Gregory had been obliged to sell Coole Park to the Forestry Department two years previously, though allowed to occupy it for the rest of her life. In the poem Lady Gregory emerges as the embodiment of traditional social and spiritual values, which had provided stability for so long. Although the house itself cannot defy time, the values it represents can, and the 'dance-like glory that those walls begot' remains as a rallying-point:

> Here, traveller, scholar, poet, take your stand
> When all those rooms and passages are gone,
> When nettles wave upon a shapeless mound
> And saplings root among the broken stone.

The realistic optimism and hope of these lines is very touching, but it is modified in the next poem on Coole Park, *Coole Park and Ballylee, 1931*, where the cruel erosion of time is seen as a challenge to poets, which they are not facing up to:

> Where fashion or mere fantasy decrees
> We shift about—all that great glory spent—
> Like some poor Arab tribesman and his tent.

'All is changed' now, and the traditional Romantic themes, 'sanctity and loveliness', are too fragile to survive in a 'darkening' age. The poet must be masterful, a horseman, controlling time rather than being swept along by it. In these two poems, then, Yeats accepts the passing of Coole Park and pays a last tribute to it, but now that Coole Park has gone he is more fully aware of the responsibilities of his imagination to recreate positive values for a new age.

Up to this point in the volume, three possibilities have been rehearsed: time can be defeated by the power of the poetic Imagination; time can be controlled by the force of tradition or personality, as exemplified by Lady Gregory; or time can uproot man. This last possibility is explored in *Coole Park and Ballylee, 1931* but it is soon dismissed as a defeatist thought. But, of course, Yeats is aware of the dangers implicit in this concept of a powerful, controlling Imagination. The Imagination must serve humanity, but in its pride it is constantly trying to evade its human responsibilities and dedicate itself to purely aesthetic pursuits. It is this problem which Yeats explores in *Byzantium*. Here the Imagination is given its head, as it were, and allowed to create a beautiful, timeless world which is apparently completely independent of humanity. Thus in the first stanza the representatives of ordinary human life, the noisy soldiers and prostitutes, are sent packing, and the poem presents a scene of purely aesthetic perfection:

> A starlit or a moonlit dome disdains
> All that man is,
> All mere complexities,
> The fury and the mire of human veins.

The very arrangement of the lines here contradicts what is ostensibly being said. 'All that man is', standing alone, defies the connotations of 'disdains' and asserts the power and variety of human life. As yet, however, this is just a hint, and in the second stanza Yeats is confronted with an inhabitant of this perfect world, a ghost who knows the mysteries of human life and can control it, can unwind the winding path of life. Excited, the poet summons this ghost, and it reveals to him the wonders of Byzantium:

> I hail the superhuman;
> I call it death-in-life and life-in-death.

The cryptic ambiguity of the second line, and the irony suggested by the journalistic 'superhuman' develop the hint of an allegiance to humanity dropped in the first stanza. The question of whether this experience is death-in-life or life-in-death, or both, is left deliberately open. The golden bird of the third stanza is deliberately dissociated from Nature and man, though the dissociation can only be comparative. It is 'more miracle than bird or handiwork', but the 'more' suggests that his aesthetic world cannot be completely independent of the real world. The 'complexities of mire or blood', 'all that man is', are scorned by this timeless aesthetic creation in the next stanza, but the fourth stanza reveals a logical flaw in this aesthetic and spiritual arrogance: this world is made for 'blood-begotten spirits' and even if they can forget and scorn their past lives on their arrival, they have to reach Byzantium first. They arrive on dolphins' backs, the traditional way, but what are the dolphins but 'mire and blood'? The dolphins are physically alive when they reach Byzantium, and they bring with them a cargo not only of spirits but of images of the real world:

> Astraddle on the dolphin's mire and blood,
> Spirit after spirit! The smithies break the flood.
> The golden smithies of the Emperor!
> Marbles of the dancing floor
> Break bitter furies of complexity,
> Those images that yet
> Fresh images beget,
> That dolphin-torn, that gong-tormented sea.

'Mire and blood' echoes 'the fury and the mire of human veins' of the first stanza, and in this stanza the aesthetic world is besieged and finally overwhelmed by the natural world. At first the flood of life is held back by 'the golden smithies' and by works of art, 'marbles of the dancing floor', but the 'bitter furies of complexity' are remorseless in their advance. The syntax conveys superbly the hopelessness of the struggle of art against life. Although the main verb 'break' is repeated, the cumulative forces of life are suggested by the apposition of the last four lines, so that the last three lines ignore the force of 'break' and assert their independent existence, just as 'all that man is' defies the connotations of 'disdains' in the first stanza. At the end, 'the unpurged images', which had only 'receded' in the first stanza, have re-established themselves in Byzantium. This meaning is reinforced by the fact that through several drafts of the poem 'fresh images' of the penultimate line appeared as 'worse images'. The poem ends, then, in the world of generation. In a sense this is a great poem because it fails to fulfil its initial purpose. Yeats's famous correspondence with the artist who did the cover design for *The Tower*, T. Sturge Moore, proves that the poem began as an attempt to overcome Moore's acute remark about *Sailing to Byzantium* that since the bird on the golden bough sang 'of what is past, or passing, or to come' it was not 'out of nature', as the poem asserted. Thus in *Byzantium* Yeats set out to create a purely aesthetic and spiritual world, but he could not do it. Life is not purged so easily, as Yeats himself had advised Anne Gregory in the charmingly avuncular *For Anne Gregory*. Art is dependent on life, however tenuous it tries to make the connection; beauty is not separable from its embodiment:

> . . . only God, my dear,
> Could love you for yourself alone
> And not your yellow hair.

For Anne Gregory and *Byzantium* are very similar in content, therefore, though very dissimilar in tone and poetic method, and yet another Yeatsian tone is used, that of anti-religious shock tactics, in *The Mother of God*. Mary is shown bewildered by her vast responsibilities, and unhappy to have been denied the ordinary satisfactions of life, 'the shows/Every common woman knows'. Rather as he had in *Leda and the Swan*, Yeats puts the cosmic, the divine, the awe-inspiring in human terms, as Mary asks in the last stanza:

> What is this flesh I purchased with my pains,
> This fallen star my milk sustains,
> This love that makes my heart's blood stop
> Or strikes a sudden chill into my bones
> And bids my hair stand up?

Perhaps God asked too much of Mary? Whatever His intention, she cannot, and will not, deny her humanity. Ordinary 'unpurged' life is still important to her:

> Chimney corner, garden walk,
> Or rocky cistern where we tread the clothes
> And gather all the talk.

In *Vacillation* Yeats explicitly asks 'What is joy?' and shows that it is in fact achieved through a fusion of body and spirit, which may be very brief, 'twenty minutes more or less' (Section IV), but which is preferable to the kind of stasis offered by religion. 'Man's blood-sodden heart' is his inspiration and his theme, and as a poet he prefers to align himself with Homer—'What theme had Homer but original sin?'—rather than Von Hügel. The final section is addressed to Von Hügel, the Roman Catholic author of *The Mystical Element of Religion*. Yeats says that he finds Von Hügel's emphasis on the miraculous aspects of religion very congenial, but he still cannot bring himself to accept religious relief from vacillation. Religion reconciles elements which through their conflict can produce a moment of visionary enlightenment such as that described in Section IV, and Yeats prefers vacillation to reconciliation:

> I—though heart might find relief
> Did I become a Christian man and choose for my belief
> What seems most welcome in the tomb—play a predestined part.
> Homer is my example and his unchristened heart.
> The lion and the honeycomb, what has Scripture said?
> So get you gone, Von Hügel, though with blessings on your head.
>
> VACILLATION VIII

Yeats is so confident that he can afford to patronise the religious philosopher, and indeed he scores a very effective point when he asks mischievously: 'The lion and the honeycomb, what has Scripture said?' Sweetness, as in the riddle Samson solved, comes from the body. 'Without contraries is no progression': Blake's dictum once more lies behind Yeats's expression of continuing faith. Now, of course, this faith is more confident because of his awareness of the possibilities of a visionary blaze which comes from the friction of opposites:

> While on the shop and street I gazed
> My body of a sudden blazed;
> And twenty minutes more or less
> It seemed, so great my happiness,
> That I was blessed and could bless.

IV

The ultimate source of this confidence is *A Vision*, and Yeats makes his debt explicit in *Gratitude to the Unknown Instructors*:

> What they undertook to do
> They brought to pass;
> All things hang like a drop of dew
> Upon a blade of grass.

The confidence is almost serene: the truth is there to be seen, though never to be grasped permanently, because of man's impure or 'fanatic' heart. This is the point made by this poem, and by the two that follow it to end the volume, *Remorse for Intemperate Speech* and *Stream and Sun at Glendalough*. As he was to say later, man can embody the truth but he cannot know it, and any attempt to know it rather than embody it that is made by the meddling intellect will distort the truth. Moments of vision must be accepted without analysis, and so the volume ends with implicit self-rebuke similar to that of the final questions of *Among School Children*. These questions about the source of a moment of happiness in natural beauty are absurdly prosaic and misguided, the products of the intellect:

> What motion of the sun or stream
> Or eyelid shot the gleam
> That pierced my body through?
> What made me live like these that seem
> Self-born, born anew?

STREAM AND SUN AT GLENDALOUGH

The answer hangs like a drop of dew upon a blade of grass, defying our grasp and our analysis.

The two most frequent words in *The Winding Stair and Other Poems* are probably 'intricate' and 'bless', and this indicates the volume's central meaning. Everything that lives in its fullness, complexity and intricacy is holy, and can bless a man if he accepts it unquestioningly. The unmentioned hero of the book is Blake's 'Natural Man', on whom Yeats, remaking himself as always, is modelling himself. In *Words for Music Perhaps* Yeats explores these ideas further through the creation who epitomises all these natural energies, Crazy Jane.

It has already been noticed that, from about 1917 onwards, women were very important in Yeats's poetry because of their comparative freedom from intellectual entanglements, and such a figure as Sheba from his earlier poetry anticipates Crazy Jane. It is characteristic of his later period, however, that Yeats should take his heroine not from the Bible but from his own observation. Crazy Jane was part of Ireland, and yet she was also outside society, thus having ample scope for her acidulous and scurrilous comments on 'the old bitter world where they marry in churches', as Yeats had seen it through the collar-bone of a hare, from the world of the dead, thirteen years previously. The importance of Crazy Jane is that she is intensely alive; she knows what she is talking about from an experience of life which has given her wisdom without bitterness. The Crazy Jane poems were started in the spring of 1929 after a period of personal depression and inactivity, and his description in a letter of the source of this new inspiration suggests his delight and gratitude:

Crazy Jane is more or less founded on an old woman who lives in a cottage near Gort. She loves her flower garden. She has just sent Lady Gregory some flowers in spite of the season and has amazing powers of acidulous speech—one of her queer performances is a description of how the meanness of a Gort shopkeeper's wife over the price of a glass of porter made her so despairing of the human race she got drunk. The incidents of the drunkenness are of an epic magnificence. She is the local satirist and a really terrible one.
LETTERS, pp. 785–6

Crazy Jane (or 'Cracked Mary' as she is called in early versions of the poems) embodies all the natural energies of humanity pitting themselves vehemently against all that restricts or forbids their expression, most notably conventional religion and the abstract intellect. There was, of course, nothing of this anti-religious feeling in the real-life character, and this element probably reflects Yeats's feelings in the months after he had been more or less ousted from the Senate by the Catholic group. The magnificent encounters between Crazy Jane and the Bishop echo very distantly, over a space of forty years, the seminal encounter between Oisin and St. Patrick, and also the more recent dialogue between self and soul. Like Yeats in *A Dialogue of Self and Soul*, Crazy Jane, looking back over her life, feels no remorse in spite of the Bishop's exhortations, but forgives herself the lot. She epitomises so much of Yeats's thought, and one could thus see her as a kind of Cuchulain figure—reflecting Yeats's presentation in his play *On Baile's Strand* (1904) of the wild heroism of Cuchulain—which could not be confined within a conventional moral or social code. Such comparisons are marginal, however, for the essential fact about Crazy Jane is her fullness of life: she is rammed with life. Jane is 'crazy' in a literal sense, being, to quote the dictionary definition 'full of cracks or flaws' after a long and full life. The poems show that she is not by any means crazy in the normally accepted sense of that word. Apparently worn out by life, an easy prey for the Bishop, she reacts angrily against conventional advice, preferring the realities of the emotions and the senses as she remembers them to promises of heavenly glory. In the face of the Bishop's advice, she asserts that man (and woman) is both body and soul, that emotional and physical experiences can have a spiritual value, though not in the Bishop's limited sense of the spirit:

> I had wild Jack for a lover;
> Though like a road
> That men pass over
> My body makes no moan
> But sings on:
> *All things remain in God.*

CRAZY JANE ON GOD

'All things', 'all that man is', express God, not just the spirit, so that physical decrepitude is no reason for 'moaning'. The poem that expresses these themes most dramatically, being the only direct verbal confrontation of Jane and the Bishop, is *Crazy Jane talks with the Bishop* in which Jane replies to the Bishop's exhortation to 'live in a heavenly mansion,/Not in some foul sty' with a magnificent assertion of the indivisible wholeness of human experience:

'Fair and foul are near of kin,
And fair needs foul,' I cried.
'My friends are gone, but that's a truth
Nor grave nor bed denied,
Learned in bodily lowliness
And in the heart's pride.

A woman can be proud and stiff
When on love intent;
But Love has pitched his mansion in
The place of excrement;
For nothing can be sole or whole
That has not been rent.'

The final paradox claims that the idea of wholeness depends on the prior existence of varied experience. The whole is produced through the fusion of parts; and this fusion is an emotional, not a conceptual one. The Bishop thinks in Either/Or terms; Jane in Both/And terms. It has often been pointed out that the central idea of this poem owes something to a line in Blake's *Jerusalem*: 'For I will make their places of love and joy excrementitious.' The poem is, in spite of this, unmistakably Yeatsian. The verbal shock of 'pitched his mansion' for example, conveys Jane's attitude that Love's mansion is not a permanent edifice, like a 'heavenly mansion', but is mobile, constantly shifting so as to follow the vagaries of human emotions. Again, the omission of the article in 'nor grave nor bed denied' suggests how fundamental Jane's view of life is. In a poem such as this the ballad form is given new life, as an unmistakably modern experience is expressed with timeless simplicity. In all the Crazy Jane poems the emotions are seen as the source of truth, as when, in *Crazy Jane Grown Old Looks at the Dancers*, Jane finds herself so caught up in the emotional drama of the dance that a precise interpretation of the dance's meaning becomes irrelevant:

Did he die or did she die?
Seemed to die or died they both?
God be with the times when I
Cared not a thraneen for what chanced
So that I had the limbs to try

> Such a dance as there was danced—
> *Love is like the lion's tooth.*

'The heart cannot lie' is the gist of these poems, and their supreme achievement is to present frankly sexual love in human terms, to invest it with a realistic tenderness which never degenerates into sentimentality. The opening lines of one of Yeats's favourite poems among his own work, *Lullaby*, illustrates this achievement:

> Beloved, may your sleep be sound
> That have found it where you fed.

The shock of the sensual 'fed' gives these opening lines an emotional complexity which is explored and defined in the poem itself and which culminates in the final lines:

> Such a sleep and sound as fell
> Upon Eurotas' grassy bank
> When the holy bird, that there
> Accomplished his predestined will,
> From the limbs of Leda sank
> But not from her protecting care.

In these lines the connotations of 'predestined will' and 'protecting care' collide and then synthesise to give an insight into the fullness and depth of Yeats's sense of human relationship. It seems possible that Auden learned this technique from Yeats, for he achieves a very similar effect in the lines:

> Lay your sleeping head, my love,
> Human on my faithless arm.

LULLABY by Auden

Here the word 'faithless' modifies what has gone before, just as 'fed' does in Yeats's lines, and both poets are distinguished by this awareness of the complexity of human emotions, the quality of Donne-like 'wit' which has nothing to do with humour.

This volume is, characteristically, concerned to express and explore a dialectic, and *Mad as the Mist and Snow* shows the new ballad simplicity being used in a poem on Yeats's perennial theme: art or life? spirit or body? Indeed, in many of the poems in this volume Yeats expresses with radical simplicity the same basic themes which he had stated in more difficult terms in his earlier work. As he says in a letter of this period, the old passion is here felt as new. The first two stanzas show two old men trying to cut themselves off from a world they no longer understand or wish to understand. As a substitute for the world they intend to glut themselves on a feast of reading, glancing contemptuously back at their youths when they were mere 'unlettered lads'. They are denying their past life, but the speaker is unable to sustain his denial:

> You ask what makes me sigh, old friend,
> What makes me shudder so?
> I shudder and I sigh to think
> That even Cicero
> And many-minded Homer were
> *Mad as the mist and snow.*

The anticipated cultural pleasures are shattered by the sudden realisation that these very books in which they are trying to bury themselves are the products of human emotions. The dramatic force of the poem depends on the change of meaning that the refrain undergoes in the final stanza. In the first two stanzas this refrain is a contemptuous rejection of life as shapeless and meaningless, but in the final stanza the forces of life are seen to be irresistible. Any art or literature that is worth bothering with leads back to life, not away from it. As T. S. Eliot has put it, literature is not an escape from life but an escape into life. Thus the old man sighs and shudders; there is no escaping life, least of all perhaps in art and literature.

The two men of *Mad as the Mist and Snow* are, of course, intellectuals, and 'monuments of unageing intellect' are a great temptation to abandon life. Thus, in this book, the most outright and explicit assertion of faith in life comes from Tom the Lunatic who agrees with Crazy Jane that all things remain in God, that human emotions have a permanence that defies Time and change:

> 'Whatever stands in field or flood,
> Bird, beast, fish or man,
> Mare or stallion, cock or hen,
> Stands in God's unchanging eye
> In all the vigour of its blood;
> In that faith I live or die.'

TOM THE LUNATIC

Perhaps Tom's most daring statement of his faith comes in *Tom at Cruachan* when, echoing one of Blake's aphorisms, he says:

> The stallion Eternity
> Mounted the mare of Time,
> 'Gat the foal of the world.

Man, in other words, is poised between Eternity and Time, and his humanity depends upon his maintaining contact with both. Man denies his humanity when he tires of the tension between these two impulses within him. As if anticipating a charge of glorifying ignorance by locating his ideal of humanity in two characters such as Crazy Jane and Tom the Lunatic, Yeats ends the volume with a poem in praise of a philosopher, Plotinus, whom he sees as having resisted the temptation to escape from life into the bland detachment of philosophy:

> Behold that great Plotinus swim,
> Buffeted by such seas;
> Bland Rhadamanthus beckons him,
> But the Golden Race looks dim,
> Salt blood blocks his eyes.

THE DELPHIC ORACLE UPON PLOTINUS

'Salt blood' suggests very strikingly how Plotinus is immersed in human problems, so that his is a human rather than transcendental philosophy. Philosophy *need* not be ethereal, any more than the life of the emotions need be bestial. Plotinus on the one hand, and Crazy Jane and Tom the Lunatic on the other, achieve this balance between Time and Eternity, Body and Soul.

In *A Woman Young and Old*, the sexual theme becomes explicit again, as a symbol of the fusion of body and spirit. Through the sexual act men and women can defeat time without forsaking their humanity. As *Chosen* says, in that moment of 'stillness . . . where his heart my heart did seem', the tyranny of sequential time is defeated: 'The Zodiac is changed into a sphere.' Perhaps the greatest difficulty a writer encounters in dealing with a sexual theme is to avoid becoming pompous or didactic. The poem *Consolation* shows how easily Yeats avoids these dangers. Once again, as in *A Dialogue of Self and Soul*, the attitude rejected is the one that thinks of birth as a crime, though Yeats admits that this pessimism has certain intellectual attractions: 'O but there is wisdom/In what the sages said.' However, talking to a beloved woman, he asks her to excuse him while he thanks the sages for providing him with the pessimism whose rejection intensifies his sexual joys:

> How could passion run so deep
> Had I never thought
> That the crime of being born
> Blackens all our lot?
> But where the crime's committed
> The crime can be forgot.

The supreme confidence of the last two lines reflects the depth of Yeats's convictions, avoiding, through the trace of wit, any suggestion of moral self-righteousness.

The positive, defiant disregard of old age shown in the Crazy Jane poems is also reflected in poems in this volume which are more specifically about old age. 'Bodily decrepitude' is seen not as a final sign of emotional exhaustion, but rather as a cloak that can, if allowed to, hide a man's permanent and unfading emotions even from himself. The emotional and human tragedy that can result from this situation is beautifully expressed in *Meeting*, where an old man and woman, lovers in their youth, greet each other with defensive scorn on meeting, repudiating the emotions of their youth:

> Hidden by old age awhile
> In masker's cloak and hood,
> Each hating what the other loved,
> Face to face we stood.

They both hate their own bodies, but still, though neither will admit it, love the body and spirit of the other: 'Each hating what the other loved.' This line, in its intense compression, is typical of this poem's tragic insight. They pour scorn on each other in their pride and rage, but the woman sees the situation as it is:

> But such as he for such as me—
> Could we both discard
> This beggarly habiliment—
> Had found a sweeter word.

This then for Yeats is the greatest temptation of old age, to be deceived by bodily decrepitude into the illogical and tragic conclusion that one is old emotionally. It is a deception that Yeats never ceased to rage against.

The poems of *A Full Moon in March* were published in 1935. The volume begins with a series of poems that prove Yeats's continuing political passions, and then comes a poem that illustrates very well the unique defiance of Yeats's poetic old age, *A Prayer for Old Age*. It begins with monosyllabic passion, deliberately exploiting the spluttering awkwardness of the first two words:

> God guard me from those thoughts men think
> In the mind alone.

The poem must be the most outspoken statement of aestheticism ever. He says that great poetry is written only by those who 'think in a marrow bone', who experience life with their whole being, and so he prays that he may be spared the conventional virtues of old age, 'all that makes a wise old man/That can be praised of all', because these virtues preclude conflict, and without conflict there can be no poetry. He knows that he will seem foolish to others, but that is a negligible price to pay for the continuing ability to write poetry:

> O what am I that I should not seem
> For the song's sake a fool?

Here Yeats's conception of poetry is shaping his life, but only because of his conviction that great poetry is the product of a great life. Here is one of Yeats's most convincing demonstrations of his refusal to separate life and art. He could not face the prospect of writing poetry which was not backed up by a full life.

The heart of this volume is *Supernatural Songs*, written in the summer of 1934. The title is, of course, partly ironic, for the very idea of the supernatural was anathema to Yeats. Professor Ellmann has expressed the central theme of these poems very effectively: 'Where Crazy Jane usually maintains that there is a spiritual aspect to physical delight, Ribh defends the converse.' Ribh, an Irish hermit, is presented by Yeats as an example of very early Christian thought, which still retains traces of pre-Christian mythology and robustness, and he is set over against St. Patrick, representing the kind of other-worldly, completely unphysical, Christianity that Yeats hated. Ribh the hermit, then, is the possessor of a Christianity which sees so-called supernatural events in human terms, showing that there is a physical aspect to spiritual delight. Thus, in *Ribh at the Tomb of Baile and Aillinn*, Ribh celebrates the passion of the pagan lovers who, on being falsely told of each other's death, had died of broken hearts. Their love is now spiritual:

> For the intercourse of angels is a light
> Where for its moment both seem lost, consumed.

Ribh, with his aquiline eyes, is not lost or consumed or blinded by this light, however. He is in no danger of idealising the 'supernatural', being aware of the constant interpenetration of the natural and supernatural, body and spirit, Time and Eternity. Indeed, he is so far from being awed by this angelic intercourse, that he uses the light it generates to read by:

> Though somewhat broken by the leaves, that light
> Lies in a circle on the grass; therein
> I turn the pages of my holy book.

Perhaps the supreme stroke is the suggestion of a complaint: the light is somewhat broken by the leaves! Ribh, in fact, has a proper grasp of the relation between the supernatural and the natural, and is thus appalled by the doctrine he hears from Patrick of an all-male Trinity. This, he says, is not supernatural, but unnatural:

> Natural and supernatural with the self-same ring are wed.
> As man, as beast, as an ephemeral fly begets, Godhead begets
> Godhead.
>
> RIBH DENOUNCES PATRICK

On this point of doctrine, Ribh clearly prefers his pre-Christian theology. Proceeding with his criticism of Christianity, Ribh says, in *Ribh Considers Christian Love Insufficient*, that Christian love can too easily degenerate into sentimentality. Man should be capable of feeling every emotion towards God, even hatred. Only thus can he achieve a complete relationship, a complete absorption in God such as is described in the last stanza. An ecstatic experience of God is one which involves the whole man, including every aspect of his body and mind, and in this sense it 'cannot endure/A bodily or mental furniture'. Ribh expresses this ecstatic absorption in God thus:

> What can she take until her Master give!
> Where can she look until He make the show!
> What can she know until He bid her know!
> How can she live till in her blood He live!

God can become real for man only when he is treated as real, and thus, paradoxically, 'Hatred of God may bring the soul to God'. Pre-eminently, then, Ribh's view of the supernatural is a common-sense one. He has a proper respect for the human as well as the superhuman.

It is clear that the driving force behind these poems is Yeats's continuing search for an all-inclusive reality. The last poem in the volume, *Meru* (named after India's Holy Mountain), expresses Yeats's sense that this search *must* be an unending and continuing one, each age undoing what a previous age has done. In spite of the apparent hopelessness of the search, every individual is committed to it, and though he may never know the truth, he may embody it:

> . . . but man's life is thought,
> And he, despite his terror, cannot cease
> Ravening through century after century,
> Ravening, raging, and uprooting that he may come
> Into the desolation of reality:

This passage is echoed in his broadcast, 'Modern Poetry', of October 1936:

> I think profound philosophy must come from terror. . . . Whether we will or no we must ask the ancient questions: Is there reality anywhere? Is there a God? Is there a Soul?

Indeed, it is Yeats's greatest strength that he is content to ask these ancient questions again and again in the hope that the intensity of his questions might some day enable him to find his own reality.

In the three volumes of poetry considered in this chapter, Yeats's search for truth becomes increasingly introspective and more intensely honest. The intensity of this poetry is that of Blake, and is well described in the passage from *A Vision* in which he catalogues the qualities that characterise Blake and other members of the Sixteenth Phase:

> There is always an element of frenzy, and almost always a delight in certain glowing or shining images of concentrated force: in the smith's forge; in the heart; in the human form in its most vigorous development; in the solar disc; in some symbolical representation of the sexual organs; for the being must brag of its triumph over its own incoherence.

The 'ravening, raging, and uprooting' that begins in this period of his poetry becomes even more self-critical in the next, and last, phase of his poetry and life, as, like Ribh, he searches for an inclusive reality that, he feels, has so far eluded him.

6

Last Judgments: 1935–1939

Right up to his death in January 1939 Yeats had frequent bursts
of frantic energy, in spite of the many ailments of the last
years—kidney trouble, heart weakness, general breathlessness
among them. Nor did his talent for friendship and appetite for
new experiences desert him. In the first year of this period, Yeats
collaborated with an Indian philosopher, Sri Purohit Swami, on
a translation of the *Upanishads* and other Indian writings. This
experience strengthened Yeats's conviction that the physical and
the spiritual were immanent in each other. Throughout these years
Yeats derived a great deal, in the way of friendship and literary
opinion, from his close relationship with Lady Dorothy Wellesley, with whom he had a long correspondence and whom he
visited frequently at her home in Cornwall. Politically, too, he
was still capable of what he called a 'Fenian' rage against England
on reading Dr. Maloney's *The Forged Diaries of Roger Casement*
of 1936, which attempted to prove how low the British government had stooped in their fight against Irish independence.
Fascism, too, continued to exercise a sporadic fascination over his
mind, though within this period he gradually became dis-
illusioned with it. Another sign of his undiminished energy was
his controversial introduction and choice of poets for *The Oxford
Book of Modern Verse*, which appeared in November 1936. He
did an immense amount of reading for this project and his
opinions on the new literary experiences of the Thirties show
his continuing openness to literary experiment and innovation.
Perhaps his most controversial omission from the Oxford selec-
tion was Wilfred Owen, an omission he justified on the grounds
that passive suffering was not a proper subject for poetry, that,

as he put it to Dorothy Wellesley, 'the creative man must impose himself upon suffering' rather than merely record it.

His compulsive desire to communicate, to 'move the common people', as he put it, remained with him to the end. Thus he was particularly delighted with an article on his poetry that appeared in the Spring 1938 number of *The Yale Review* because the writer, Archibald MacLeish, spoke of the language of his poetry as being 'public'. Writing to Lady Dorothy Wellesley, he says of this praise: 'That word which I had not thought of myself is a word I want.' He disagreed with the article's contention that this public language might most profitably have been used on political themes, for he saw politics as essentially fraudulent and superficial, 'the manipulation of popular enthusiasm by false news', a view he expresses again in the poem *Politics*. He saw his essential task as being the pursuit of essential truths about the unique nature of human life; and his publication in 1937 of a radically revised edition of *A Vision*, which hinted at the existence of God, shows that he thought of his philosophical and mystical speculations as being a very important part of this pursuit. Perhaps the central symbolic events of these last years were the four broadcasts on his own and modern poetry which he gave for the B.B.C. between October 1936 and October 1937. His enthusiasm for artistic and technical details and his delight in the possibilities of communication opened up by broadcasting were so intense that he found broadcasting physically exhausting, and he had to give it up, reluctantly, after October 1937. The same desire to communicate, to make himself understood to all, lies behind his idea of a periodical, to be called *On the Boiler*, which he broached in late 1937: 'some when they see my meaning set out in plain print will hate me for poems which they had thought meant nothing.' If the public would not make the effort necessary to an understanding of his poetry, then he would put it in prosaic terms: he insisted on being understood.

Above all, however, this was a period of judgment, on himself and his work particularly, but in these last poems he surveys, using the theories of *A Vision* as a framework, the whole of modern civilisation as he sees it. The poems of these years have a judicial sweep which makes them quite different from the poems of the Crazy Jane and Ribh period. As always, he was particularly exacting and acute in his self-criticism as, surveying his work, he asks whether it has done justice to the complexities of life. His resumed meetings with Maud Gonne in these years prompted him to 'follow to its source/Every event in action or in thought' which had concerned his relationship with her and, through her, with Ireland. Looking back over his life and work he tries to find some pattern in them and increasingly he defines the proper response to life and suffering in terms of an exultant gaiety. Throughout his life he had tried to make sense of life without distorting it, and the emotion of tragic joy felt by the great tragic heroes now appears to him as the only possible final, positive response to life. Writing of Shakespeare's heroes, he says that they are 'reborn in gaiety' after their suffering and thus achieve a kind of mastery over it. 'Joy' and 'gaiety' are two of the most frequent words in his poetry and prose of this period, and his views are very succinctly expressed in a letter to Dorothy Wellesley: 'Joy is the salvation of the soul.' In another letter, of 1935, he says: 'I want to make a last song, sweet and exultant.' Having experienced, like the great tragic heroes, extreme suffering and doubt, he now achieves the equipoise of joy and gaiety, though, inevitably with Yeats, there are doubts even about this state.

Certainly he never felt that he had stated his final truth, for he went on writing poetry almost to the day of his death. He finished his revision of *Under Ben Bulben* on 27 January, and died in Mentone, where he was spending the winter, on 28 January 1939. His last volume of poetry was *New Poems* of 1938, and these poems are grouped with others from this final period in *Last Poems*, which was published posthumously. A remark in a letter of November 1935, in which he says that a poet must avoid propaganda above all else, establishes the mood of the period very well: 'three important persons know nothing of it [propaganda]—a man modelling a statue, a man playing a flute, and a man in a woman's arms.' These important persons know joy, and most of these last poems are songs of exultant joy.

Last Poems begins with *The Gyres* which is, in effect, an injunction to the poet himself to look out over the whole of human life, and its prevailing desolation, and to rejoice. Once again, Yeats tests the validity of his poetic imagination by making it look at life and its suffering. His response this time seems at first almost callous: 'We that look on but laugh in tragic joy.' The key-word, of course, is 'tragic'. This joy arises not from callousness or insouciance but from an awareness of the permanence of the best aspects of humanity, in spite of their apparent destruction. Expressing this awareness in his own terms, Yeats says that the gyres of history will 'disinter' nobility, beauty and tradition again because these are not qualities of a particular age, but permanent, indestructible qualities of the human mind. The poet, too, has suffered, so that he is now 'Old Rocky Face'. His joy has behind it the sanction of personal experience, but his memories are not bitter. Now that he trusts in the future course of history he need no longer rage against the destroyers of what he values, nor shout the praises of those he loves, and this new control and confidence are reflected in such a line as 'Hector is dead and there's a light in Troy', which suggests his almost matter-of-fact acceptance of destruction as one necessary part of the cycles of civilisation. This is something new in Yeats. The sentiment, 'Conduct and work grow coarse, and coarse the soul,/What matter?', though recognisable for the most part as a characteristically Yeatsian sentiment would not have been expressed with such assurance in Yeats's earlier work.

The next poem in this volume, *Lapis Lazuli* of July 1936, presents the same theme, but in more specifically aesthetic terms. Tragic gaiety is set over against the hysteria of women's speculation about a future war, and again Yeats surveys past civilisations, finding a constant pattern of construction and destruction:

> All things fall and are built again,
> And those that build them again are gay.

This tragic gaiety, then, is not a static attitude; it carries within itself the impetus to reconstruct what it has seen destroyed. The final section of the poem expresses Yeats's viewpoint symbolically. A Chinese carving in lapis lazuli presents two Chinamen and a serving man viewing dispassionately the ruin that surrounds them. No doubt, Yeats implies, when the carving was first made they were surrounded by a more congenial scene, but time has ravaged the inessential aspects of the carving:

> Every discoloration of the stone,
> Every accidental crack or dent,
> Seems a water-course or an avalanche,
> Or lofty slope where it still snows.

What has survived, however, is the attitude they represent, the tragic wisdom that can accept rise and fall with joy:

> Their eyes mid many wrinkles, their eyes,
> Their ancient, glittering eyes, are gay.

The wrinkles testify that their gaiety is not the gaiety of irresponsibility, but of tragic insight.

In the next two poems, *Imitated from the Japanese* and *Sweet Dancer*, Yeats returns to one of his favourite symbols, that of the dancer, and gives it an extra layer of meaning that makes it fit into the context of this volume. Like the men in the lapis lazuli carving, the dancer achieves a stasis and equilibrium which go beyond suffering, make her in a sense impregnable, and so the second poem finishes:

> If strange men come from the house
> To lead her away, do not say
> That she is happy being crazy;
> Lead them gently astray;
> Let her finish her dance,
> Let her finish her dance.
> *Ah, dancer, ah, sweet dancer!*

Her happiness is not that of craziness but of tragic joy. But this tragic joy and gaiety can come only to those who have experienced the whole of life, so the next poem, *The Three Bushes*, is in a sense a cautionary tale about those who shrink from a total involvement in life. It begins with a brilliantly lucid narrative of a plan conceived by a lady to save herself from what she considers would be the degradation of sexual love with the man she claims to love. The plan is to substitute her maid for herself in her lover's bed at night, and this plan seems to work up to a point. However, when her lover is accidentally killed hurrying to join her, as he thinks, she dies of remorse, 'for she/Loved him with her soul'. The logic of the poem requires, of course, that the chambermaid's love should be seen as genuine, and this proves to be the case, for when she confesses to a priest her part in the plan, he recognises her genuine emotions, and on her death has her buried alongside the graves of her former mistress and her lover. Each grave has a rose-bush planted on it, and in time the three bushes intermingle:

> And now none living can,
> When they have plucked a rose there,
> Know where its roots began.

After death the three people achieve union of a kind that was denied them, through the lady's folly, during their lives. Thus the heart of the poem is 'The Lady's Second Song', one of six songs that follow the actual narrative. The Lady expresses her misguided views to the maid in these ominous terms:

> He shall love my soul as though
> Body were not at all,
> He shall love your body
> Untroubled by the soul,
> Love cram love's two divisions
> Yet keep his substance whole.

This division of love prevents a full experience of life for any of the poem's characters, and so they are overwhelmed by events over which they have no control. And the Lady and the chambermaid are denied the tragic joy which might have helped them to understand these events.

The tragic view of life must be total, without any preconceived limits, and in *An Acre of Grass* Yeats rages against the limits that society seeks to impose on old men. He will not be put out to pasture on an acre of green grass, he says, but will model himself on those figures, from art as well as life, who retained their creative frenzy into old age:

> Grant me an old man's frenzy,
> Myself must I remake
> Till I am Timon and Lear
> Or that William Blake
> Who beat upon the wall
> Till Truth obeyed his call;
>
> A mind Michael Angelo knew
> That can pierce the clouds,
> Or inspired by frenzy
> Shake the dead in their shrouds;
> Forgotten else by mankind,
> An old man's eagle mind.

What he is insisting on here is his right, in spite of old age, to experience the whole of life, to pierce the clouds or shake the dead in their shrouds, and this idea of the importance of total experience is presented in *Beautiful Lofty Things* and *A Crazed Girl*. In these poems he presents, first, a static vision of figures from his past life (*Beautiful Lofty Things*) and then a vision of a 'crazed girl' glimpsed dancing amid the prosaic surroundings of a dock: like the figures described in the first poem, she too is 'a beautiful lofty thing'. Loftiness, beauty, nobility can be found in any setting, and in the glimpse of the dancing girl's beauty he finds again what he had thought lost for ever:

> . . . that girl I declare
> A beautiful lofty thing, or a thing
> Heroically lost, heroically found.

These two poems are, in a sense, Yeats's personal testimony that the finest aspects of humanity survive their apparent destruction. At the end of *Beautiful Lofty Things*, after surveying the grandeur of his and Ireland's past, he had declared of this period's nobility, 'a thing never known again'. In *A Crazed Girl* he refutes his own pessimism, proving the truth of the gaily tragic view of life: 'All things fall and are built again.'

Probably the best known and most controversial poem from

this collection is *The Spur*, of December 1936. It is a caustic rejoinder to those, Dorothy Wellesley among them, who had expressed a slight uneasiness about the political and sexual frankness of his later poetry:

> You think it horrible that lust and rage
> Should dance attention upon my old age;
> They were not such a plague when I was young;
> What else have I to spur me into song?

'Lust and rage', the poem asserts, are not new personal qualities; they have always been the motivating force behind his poetry, though perhaps they were called something more complimentary when he was a younger man. He is saying, quite simply, that he is the same man he has always been, and he exposes with extraordinary economy the fallacy of the view that would have him behave and write differently now. In fact, of course, lust, in the normal sense of that word, is totally absent from Yeats's verse, though in its original sense of a desire to enjoy life to the full it is a very precise description of the force behind his work. Rage there certainly is throughout his work, and it appears in a political form in this volume in, for example, *The Curse of Cromwell*. Writing to Dorothy Wellesley, he says the poem is the expression of his rage against the intelligentsia—Cromwell, in his view, being the Lenin of his day. The poem attributes the decline of the way of life he had valued to what we would now call the 'rat-race', and this in its turn he traces to the influence on contemporary life of the intelligentsia, the revolutionary intellectuals who are intent only on destruction and who brutally destroy whatever impedes their intentions. As a result of their actions, the poet is now alone, tormented by his memories of a way of life which seems impossible now. Though he is tormented, he is by no means cowed, however, as the poem's refrain shows:

> O what of that, O what of that,
> What is there left to say?

Though this poem is by no means a confident assertion of the detachment of tragic gaiety, it moves towards that assertion.

The rage is so intense that it prevents tragic acceptance throughout most of the poem. In fact, of course, if the mood of tragic joy had been allowed to dominate *Last Poems* completely the volume would not be nearly so disturbing as it is. In spite of his assertion, and achievement, of tragic joy and gaiety in some poems, suffering is not always so easily transcended, nor the tragic view accepted so confidently. The equipoise of tragic joy is not an attitude that can be persisted in: it is essentially a brief glimpse of life's ultimate meaning, and Yeats was too great and honest a poet to make it a permanent attitude.

Thus his attempt to see his and Ireland's recent history in terms of fixed artistic images in *The Municipal Gallery Revisited*, of August and September 1937, is not altogether convincing. He has to recognise that what he is looking at is 'an Ireland/The poets have imagined, terrible and gay', when he looks at the paintings in the gallery, and he is honest enough to admit a gap between the images of art and the complexities of life as he remembers it. This feeling emerges with particular force in his comment on a portrait of Lady Gregory:

> Mancini's portrait of Augusta Gregory,
> 'Greatest since Rembrandt,' according to John Synge;
> A great ebullient portrait certainly;
> But where is the brush that could show anything
> Of all that pride and that humility?
> And I am in despair that time may bring
> Approved patterns of women or of men
> But not that selfsame excellence again.

Here his theories about the permanent realities of art and the cyclical recurrence of great human and social qualities are being questioned; he knows that art has limitations, that it can never express life's fullness, and he knows, too, that 'that selfsame excellence' will never be brought round again by the gyres, even though they may bring something very similar. Having expressed these doubts, he gathers, in the rest of the poem, what consolation he can from the fact that the pictures in the Municipal Gallery give some idea of his and Ireland's past, and asks the reader who would judge him to judge not just his poetry, but to come to the gallery so as to get some impression of the human and social context of his poetry. But there is a contradiction even here: he is asking the reader to use one form of art for the purpose of repairing the deficiencies of another, his poetry, and the inescapable logic of this request is that all art is at best a pale reflection of life. As he admits in the second stanza, the Ireland of his youth is irretrievably dead, and the 'permanent or impermanent images' of poetry or art can only partially redeem time. The emotional impact of the poem is that the time of happiness and stability is past, and although he says in the fifth stanza that he has not wept at the end of the Coole Park tradition, this is a direct contradiction of his description of his emotions in the third stanza:

> Heart-smitten with emotion I sink down,
> My heart recovering with covered eyes.

The greatness of this poem is that, like *Byzantium*, it fails in its intention of deriving complete consolation for the suffering of life in the timeless world of art. The tensions of the poem remind one of a comment he made in a letter to Dorothy Wellesley in August 1936:

> We have all something within ourselves to batter down and get our power from this fighting. I have never 'produced' a play in verse without showing the actors that the passion of the verse comes from the fact that the speakers are holding down violence or madness—'down Hysterica passio.' All depends on the completeness of the holding down, on the stirring of the beast underneath. . . . Without this conflict we have no passion only sentiment and thought.   LETTERS ON POETRY TO DOROTHY WELLESLEY, pp. 94–5

Powerful emotions certainly stir just beneath the surface of this poem, and occasionally emerge. It is a relief on reading this poem to recognise again the Yeatsian argument with himself, for, fine though they are in their way, the poems of tragic joy lack the power to disturb which is, perhaps, Yeats's central achievement. In view of this, it is significant that Yeats himself was very pleased with *The Municipal Gallery Revisited*, and he wrote to Dorothy Wellesley that it was 'perhaps the best poem

I have written for some years, unless the *Curse of Cromwell* is'.

Yeats's honesty makes it impossible for him to remain satisfied with tragic joy as an attitude to life, but in these years his characteristic honesty about himself and his poetry was intensified by his realisation of the imminence of death. These were years of illness and convalescence. The greatness of *Last Poems* arises from the constant alternation between confidence in the ability of art to make sense of life and a conviction that all that matters is individual experience. *The Statues*, of June 1938, is his most explicit statement of the positive, shaping influence that art can have on life. The best gloss on the poem is a passage·from *On the Boiler*:

> There are moments when I am certain that art must once again accept those Greek proportions which carry into plastic art the Pythagorean numbers, those faces which are divine because all there is empty and measured. Europe was not born when Greek galleys defeated the Persian hordes at Salamis, but when the Doric studios sent out those broad-backed marble statues against the multiform, vague, expressive Asiatic sea, they gave to the sexual instinct of Europe its goal, its fixed type.   ON THE BOILER, p. 37

Greek art, he is saying, was not subjective: it was almost mathematically exact in its proportions, but it was influential precisely because it was mathematical. Not being the expression of the artist's personal, subjective emotions, it acted as 'a fixed type', a framework within which the individual could express himself. Thus the poem begins by mentioning public incomprehension or criticism of such an objective art: people stare and say that sculpture, for example, wrought on these principles, lacks character. But young people find 'that passion could bring character enough'. Impersonal art can have a universal relevance, whereas personal art is often no more than autobiography. The assertion is familiar from *Ego Dominus Tuus*, though it is explored in much greater detail here. In the second stanza of the poem Yeats expresses his belief that the Greek sculptors, Phidias in particular, were responsible for the survival of Europe in the face of the Persian menace. In the difficult third stanza, Yeats seems to be saying that these Greek ideals also influenced Asian art, and that the compulsive attractions of the Buddha can be attributed to its Greek-like objectivity. Tragically, the stanza says, Europe has lost this objectivity in its art, as becomes clear if the Buddha is compared with the ultimate symbol of European subjectivity, morbid interest in the self, 'Hamlet thin from eating flies'. The fourth stanza is more hopeful in the suggestion that objective art, based on intellect, calculation, number and measurement, has begun once again to have a decisive and formative influence on modern Europe, in the form of the Irish nation which, Yeats suggests, was inspired to the Easter Rising by the admiration of Pearse and his followers for the objective figure of Cuchulain, symbolising the refusal to be dominated or limited by outside forces. Yeats suggests that Ireland and her artists must now follow the lead of Pearse. Through an objective art, Ireland can lift itself above the formless subjectivity of modern life and achieve its national destiny. Extraordinarily, Yeats here becomes once again an Irish poet of the school of O'Leary, though able to make a much more profound and powerful contribution to the cause of Irish nationalism than he had almost fifty years previously. A poem such as *The Statues* makes it clear that the the relation between art and life in *Last Poems* is very different from that of the Byzantium poems. Art may not *always* provide the answer in *Last Poems* but at least it does not mock man's puny efforts.

The Statues is one of Yeats's most difficult poems, both in thought and language, but solving the difficulty is rewarding. He is capable, on the other hand, of presenting a variation on the theme of this poem in very much simpler terms, as in *Long-legged Fly*. The brilliant strategy of this poem is to describe the moment of quiet concentration and intensity that preceded decisive changes in civilisation. Caesar, Helen and Michelangelo are presented pondering the future, islanded in silence, and themselves only dimly aware of the immensity of what they are contemplating. The poem's ballad refrain is probably Yeats's most effective, reiterating an image of which the relevance gradually becomes clear:

> *Like a long-legged fly upon the stream,*
> *His mind moves upon silence.*

Like the fly hovering upon the stream, these people are in time and are yet shaping it, rising above it. Thus the fly is clearly not in the stream, but there is no clear break between the fly and the stream. What distinguishes all three of these vastly influential people is their unobtrusive quietness and objectivity:

> His eyes fixed upon nothing,
> A hand under his head;

>   . . . her feet
> Practise a tinker shuffle
> Picked up on a street;

> With no more sound than the mice make
> His hand moves to and fro.

The structure of each verse reinforces this point, beginning with a subordinate clause which mentions matters of vast importance, and then going on to the main clause which contains an apparently trivial request. Thus the first stanza begins:

> That civilisation may not sink,
> Its great battle lost,
> Quiet the dog, tether the pony
> To a distant post.

The reader is immediately surprised, brought into the poem, and then the meaning is gradually made more obvious through examples. The poem goes beyond *The Statues* in suggesting that men or women of the world, artists in life, so to speak, can influence civilisation as decisively as an artist such as Michelangelo.

Yeats's final poem about Maud Gonne, *A Bronze Head*, was inspired by a sculpture by Lawrence Campbell in the Dublin Municipal Gallery. Yeats sees this image of Maud as reconciling the various contradictory aspects of her character which had always defeated his comprehension. Here she is 'human, super-human', both a 'tomb-haunter' and 'a most gentle woman'.

'Tomb-haunter' is a disparaging reference to Maud's character-istic black clothes, which symbolised her stern political con-science and purpose, the aspect of her personality which had always antagonised Yeats. Here, in the work of art, 'substance is composite', she is presented in a fullness which had always escaped him when he was with the flesh-and-blood woman. The third and fourth stanzas recall her 'wildness' and her 'supernatural' sense of national destiny, and somehow the artistic achievement of the sculpture is forgotten as Yeats is carried along by the emotion of his memories. Thus the poem ends with inconclusive abruptness, the certainties of the first two stanzas dissipated. It is the uncertainty and abruptness which make it a fine and distinctively Yeatsian poem, and the poet was clearly right to omit a confidently conclusive stanza, to be found in a draft of the poem, in which he tells himself not to brood on old triumph but to prepare for death gaily:

> . . . prepare to die.
> Even at the approach of the un-imaged night
> Man has the refuge of his gaiety.
>
> Quoted in W. B. YEATS, MAN AND POET, p. 294

As he felt death approaching—this poem was written in the summer of 1938—he saw that gaiety could be debased so that it becomes a mere 'refuge', and he preferred to face up to his 'un-imaged' emotions and past life. The images of art, he saw, can only take us so far; in the end man has to face the burdens, and rewards, of his uniqueness.

The emotional pressures, 'the stirring of the beast underneath', that led him gradually to forsake the refuge of tragic gaiety and artistic permanence, come fully to the surface in some of the poems written in the last six months of his life. *High Talk*, for example, questions once again the validity of poetry's version of reality, by presenting the poet as a kind of circus performer walking on stilts and so catching public attention, but being off the ground in every sense: 'Malachi Stilt-Jack am I.' The pres-sures and questions are controlled in this poem by a self-depracia-tory irony, such as is suggested by the matter-of-fact opening line: 'Processions that lack high stilts have nothing that catches the eye.' The doubts overwhelm the irony in the closing section, however, when the ponderous and artificial efforts of the poet to express reality are devastatingly juxtaposed to this reality itself, though, of course, the very beauty of these closing lines of the poem act as an assurance of the validity of poetry:

> All metaphor, Malachi, stilts and all. A barnacle goose
> Far up in the stretches of night; night splits and the dawn breaks
> > loose;
> I, through the terrible novelty of light, stalk on, stalk on;
> Those great sea-horses bare their teeth and laugh at the dawn.

Thus, paradoxically, a poem which sets out to suggest that poetry is absurdly artificial ends by demonstrating poetry's power. Poetry and Nature need not be at odds, provided the poet gets down off his stilts.

The aspect most likely to disturb the equilibrium of tragic gaiety is impending death, and *The Apparitions* presents Yeats's awareness of death without any suggestion of a refuge from personal terror. 'Joy' is mentioned in this final stanza, but the last five lines, particularly the terrible beauty of the refrain, cancel its meaning:

> When a man grows old his joy
> Grows more deep day after day,
> His empty heart is full at length,
> But he has need of all that strength
> Because of the increasing Night
> That opens her mystery and fright.
> *Fifteen apparitions have I seen;*
> *The worst a coat upon a coat-hanger.*

It would be almost a relief to be able to speak of Yeats's final poetry as expressing a tragic stasis and equilibrium, but, as always, Yeats's ideals and ideas crack under the pressure of life's complexities, even an idea incorporating as much wisdom and insight as that of tragic gaiety. His awareness of Time's derision and cruelty never softens, and he never shirks the task of expressing it. Thus, in *Why Should not Old Men be Mad?* he looks back to Maud and Iseult and the wastefulness of their lives as he sees them, and says that some people might accept such tragedy with equanimity:

> Some think it a matter of course that chance
> Should starve good men and bad advance.

But, he says, a realisation of the inevitability of tragedy is no great comfort when the tragedy involves us as deeply as this one does Yeats. Age may teach the inevitability of tragedy, but it does not necessarily bring an understanding or acceptance of it:

> Young men know nothing of this sort,
> Observant old men know it well;
> And when they know what old books tell,
> And that no better can be had,
> Know why an old man should be mad.

This is the ravening, raging and uprooting poetry that he had mentioned in *Meru*, and it is used once more to examine his poetic career in the most judicial of his final poems, *The Circus Animals' Desertion*. Before he hit on this title, Yeats called the poem *Despair* and later *On the Lack of a Theme*. It is a poem about poetry, or more precisely about not being able to write poetry, and, as in *High Talk* but even more effectively, the writing of a poem about not being able to write poetry resolves the paradox, suggesting the kind of poetry he should now write. Yeats begins by suggesting that now he must give up poetry, and be satisfied with un-imaged life: 'Maybe at last, being but a broken man,/I must be satisfied with my heart.' All the mythology of his earlier poetry is dismissed as idealistic self-delusion, as are his early plays:

> Players and painted stage took all my love,
> And not those things that they were emblems of.
>
> THE CIRCUS ANIMALS' DESERTION

The trappings had been more important than the theme, he now recognises, and he determines to penetrate to the ultimate source of poetry and to express his emotions unadorned, without the mythological paraphernalia:

Those masterful images because complete
Grew in pure mind, but out of what began?
A mound of refuse or the sweepings of a street,
Old kettles, old bottles, and a broken can,
Old iron, old bones, old rags, that raving slut
Who keeps the till. Now that my ladder's gone,
I must lie down where all the ladders start,
In the foul rag-and-bone shop of the heart.

The masterful images of his earlier poetry are found wanting precisely because they are masterful, representing the mind's repression or distortion of human emotions. The most impressive aspect of this stanza is its cumulative emotional and rhythmic power. Because of this power, the reader is left with a heightened sense of the importance of the emotions and the heart, in spite of the description of the heart as a 'foul rag-and-bone shop'. Aesthetic purity is being rejected in favour of human foulness, and the emotional power of the poem almost reverses the normal meanings of 'pure' and 'foul'.

This mood of savage self-appraisal is touched on again and then transcended in *The Man and the Echo*. Looking back over his earlier work he wonders whether he could have written differently, and thus have changed the course of history. Speculating on this, he is tortured by doubts:

All that I have said and done,
Now that I am old and ill,
Turns into a question till
I lie awake night after night
And never get the answer right.

He is tempted to despair, to 'lie down and die', but he realises that that would be cowardly, and he is recalled from these barren suicidal speculations by a cry of suffering, which reinforces his conviction that suicide is no answer:

But hush, for I have lost the theme,
Its joy or night seem but a dream;
Up there some hawk or owl has struck,
Dropping out of sky or rock,

> A stricken rabbit is crying out,
> And its cry distracts my thought.

The Hamlet-like speculation about suicide and the after-life is forgotten and the problem of suffering and evil reassumes its primacy in Yeats's mind. As Vivienne Koch says of this passage: 'The creativity of suffering, the claims of suffering upon "life", had never been put by Yeats with such a tender pity.'

Yeats's last two poems, *The Black Tower* and *Under Ben Bulben*, are best read in conjunction, for they express both aspects of his final exploration of the relation between art and life, spirit and body. In *The Black Tower* the image of a besieged tower expresses Yeats's determination to persevere in his allegiance to a way of life and a system of values which seems doomed, rather than accept the alternatives:

> Those banners come to bribe or threaten,
> Or whisper that a man's a fool
> Who, when his own right king's forgotten,
> Cares what king sets up his rule.
> If he died long ago
> Why do you dread us so?

Yeats's determination is based on the belief, suggested in the poem's refrain, that the human qualities he admires most will re-emerge and reward his allegiance. Though the general theme is very similar to that of *The Gyres*, the tone is very different. The assurance of the earlier poem has been replaced by grim determination: 'Stand we on guard oath-bound!' This is Yeats's final poem of resisted temptation, and the temptation to swim with the tide is as urgent and attractive as ever. This is one aspect of *Last Poems*, the doubt and the tentative hope. The other aspect, the belief in the power of great poetry or art to shape a nation's destiny, to defeat time, is reaffirmed in *Under Ben Bulben*. In essence, it is a last message to Irish poets to 'sing whatever is well made' and thus achieve the art of Phidian measurement whose vast influence Yeats had asserted in *The Statues*. Such poetry or sculpture proves the 'profane perfection of mankind', and shows that death is illusory; that this profane perfection, if not its particular embodiments in any one age, is recurrent:

> Though grave–diggers' toil is long,
> Sharp their spades, their muscles strong,
> They but thrust their buried men
> Back in the human mind again.

UNDER BEN BULBEN

This confidence in the power of well-made poetry or art lies behind Yeats's own epitaph with which the poem ends:

> No marble, no conventional phrase;
> On limestone quarried near the spot
> By his command these words are cut:
> > *Cast a cold eye*
> > *On life, on death.*
> > *Horseman, pass by!*

The curtly imperious tone of these lines expresses Yeats's confidence in the kind of objective, impersonal art of which his epitaph itself is a fine example. The epitaph is a deliberate rejection of the 'conventional phrase' often carved on grave-stones, 'Siste viator', meaning 'Pause traveller'. This conventional phrase was often the prelude to lines on man's mortality, exhorting the traveller to think about the last things. But Yeats's epitaph is not cynical, as is sometimes supposed; the horseman is urged to get on with the business of living and avoid superfluous emotion. Death is not final; the human mind survives and the proper business of life is to do justice to the human mind, to show the 'profane perfection' of which man is capable. But *Under Ben Bulben* does less than justice to the range of Yeats's mind and emotions. In the last months of his life, as in all his great poetry, the kind of confidence and aspiration expressed here is only part of the argument with himself. True, art can shape life, as *Under Ben Bulben* asserts, but nevertheless each man has his own life to live and his own temptations to resist, as *The Black Tower* shows.

In *Last Poems*, Yeats's honesty and artistic integrity force him once again to recognise that any generalisation about life, however broad or wise, must by its very nature do less than justice to life's complexities, its minute particulars. These poems achieve, because of this recognition, the tension and excitement which distinguish Yeats's best poetry. As he says in *A Vision*, 'The greater the contrast the more intense the consciousness', and in *Last Poems* the perennial Yeatsian contrasts become even more intense because of his knowledge that he was exploring them for probably the last time. In 1938, writing in *On the Boiler*, Yeats praises a book by his brother because of 'his pursuit of all that through its unpredictable, unarrangeable reality, least resembles knowledge'. His suspicion of abstract knowledge is a constant trait of Yeats's character from his earliest days of 'monkish hate' for Victorian science and thought, and it is an essential part of the judicial mood of these last poems and of his last letters: 'Man can embody truth but he cannot know it'; 'The abstract is not life and everywhere draws out its contradictions.' His poetry is as fine an embodiment of truth as this century has produced, and *Last Poems* makes a distinctive contribution to its fineness by presenting him with different kinds of 'knowledge' and tempting him for the last time to take refuge in abstractions from the unpredictable, unarrangeable reality of old age.

7

Conclusion

'Was it a vision, or a waking dream?/Fled is that music:—Do I wake or sleep?' The profoundly honest and difficult questions with which Keats concludes his *Ode to a Nightingale* had a vast influence on those later poets who were attracted by the Romantic idea of a creative poetic Imagination which could transform the world and help the poet to see permanent truths through his poetic vision. Not to go too deeply into the complexities of modern poetic theory, Yeats is perhaps the greatest modern representative of Romanticism as it was defined by the English Romantics, the central figure in what has been called the 'Romantic survival' in this century. All the English Romantic poets were aware of the dangers of the Imagination—though Keats expressed the dangers most memorably—but this awareness only modified their allegiance to its powers, for they saw the alternative as mere analytical, conceptual thought which buried itself in its own intricacies, losing sight of the larger questions about poetry and human life. Thus the characteristic note of great Romantic poetry is one of uncertainty, of alternation between elation and despair, a feeling of being, now, at one with the deepest sources of life and, now, cut off from them. If comparisons between the great English Romantics and Yeats tend to focus on Keats, it is because both Keats and Yeats had an intense and dedicated view of poetry and its powers so that their misgivings about poetry, their recurrent fear that the poet was an escapist, inferior to the man of action or the social reformer, were agonised ones. They both knew that the Imagination must not be allowed to sever its connections with life, but they both found the prospect of a pure world of the Imagination very attractive because of their prodigious gifts and, more importantly, because of the pervasive unhappiness and uncertainty of their personal lives. Keats, in *The Fall of Hyperion*, and Yeats in the poetry of his last ten years or so, both expressed a belief that poetry which could not deal with the central human problem of suffering and evil was, however sublime, merely decorative; but uncertainty and temptation never completely leave them. Considering the early careers of both poets, one sees that they could both so easily have become 'poets' poets', so that their refusals to accept the various aesthetic escape routes that their backgrounds and gifts made available, and their lives desirable, are heroic resistances, not just literary but human achievements.

This study of Yeats began with the suggestion that he can best be understood in relation to his times and that the sources of his work and thought are often public rather than esoteric. One aspect of his life and work touched on only briefly in this study, his plays, shows how public a writer he was. As early as 1884, for example, he was expressing himself naturally and effectively through plays, and he continued writing for the theatre well into his old age. Though often underrated, his contribution to the Irish dramatic renaissance was a vital one, in a literary as well as a practical sense. To use his own comment on the relation between his plays and his poetry, his dramatic work often provided him with a new mass of thought and feeling that overflowed into his poetry. Thus, three such plays as *On Baile's Strand* (1904), *At the Hawk's Well* (1917) and *Resurrection* (1931) show him exploring ideas and techniques which appear at the same time or later in his poetry. Thus Cuchulain, the hero of the first play, exercised a constant fascination over him, prompting him to explore the possibilities of heroic behaviour within a general social structure, while the second play shows him suggesting the need for some compromise between prudence and reckless heroism. Similarly, *Resurrection* examines the dialectic between idealism and scepticism, suggesting again the necessity for a fusion of these qualities. However, Professor Ure's book on Yeats as a playwright does him full justice, and contains probably the most perceptive comments on the relation between his plays and his poetry. In his plays Yeats expressed his continuing idealistic hopes for a full harmony between literature and its values and the general public, while in his poetry he explored more personally and sceptically the difficulties of any such harmony, though never lapsing into pessimism.

It is precisely because Yeats was in many ways a public poet that it is so difficult to organise without distortion or simplification the materials of his genius. Yeats himself helps most here by his intelligent arrangement of his poems within the various volumes, so that they germinate out of each other, suggesting his current preoccupations and pointing out the directions a reader should take in relating his poetry to his life and times. Of course, the principle that Yeats's volumes of poetry are architectural in their structure can be a dangerous one, for his poetry is, if one can use the term, an organic architecture. Each poem must be allowed to register its own meaning before being related to its immediate context within a volume, otherwise a very useful guide to interpretation becomes a strait-jacket and the uniqueness of a particular poem is lost. Professor Jeffares, in his critical biography, has written very well on this sameness with difference of many of Yeats's poems:

> The extraordinary nature of his poetic vitality came from his ability to remodel his personality, perhaps even on a model which he had used before, but never quite in the same way.
>
> W. B. YEATS, MAN AND POET, p. 287

Yeats's best poems are unique embodiments of truth: the apparent similarity of a particular truth to some other embodied in another Yeats poem should prompt us to look more eagerly for the distinctive qualities of the poem rather than dismiss it as repetition.

This is particularly important because it is the sense of the subjective nature of Truth and the sterility of generalisations and abstractions that lies behind many of his poems. In this belief he is at one with Blake, the English Romantic he admired most, and with Coleridge's view, for example, that 'truth is the correlative of being'; that our knowledge is fundamentally personal and intuitive, that no truth exists independently of its embodiment. The object of poetry is to express the fullness of human truths through the Imagination, and the great enemy of poetry is abstractness of thought and facility of expression, all the qualities Yeats summarised in his particular meaning of 'rhetoric'.

Only now, perhaps, are we beginning to see how public and social English Romanticism was, how Wordsworth, Coleridge and Blake, in particular, must be studied against their social and political background if they are to be fully understood and appreciated. Yeats was the heir of English Romanticism in this respect, too, for he believed that the poet must speak to his age, must be a prophet rather than a priest, and it is thus very important to see Yeats's involvement in public life and controversy as being an essential part of his poetic vocation, rather than a series of incidental and irrelevant escapades. Without this sense of the social and political background to his poetry, the tendency is to place too much emphasis on *A Vision* in studying and assessing Yeats, so that this book tends to become the holy book of the Yeats critic. After all, Yeats himself never made any great claims for *A Vision* as philosophy; he spoke of its value as being a personal one for him, a scaffolding for his poetry. Through it, he saw a pattern in history which gave him tentative bearings but he was not the man ever to suggest that this was *the* pattern of history. It is here perhaps that Yeats comes closest to Donne. Donne's sense of contemporary chaos and disorientation and his search for certainty are similarly reflected in his omnivorous appetite for knowledge and in his impatience with conventions.

In view of all this, it is clear that any attempt to summarise Yeats's achievement in a phrase or sentence would have been repugnant to him, and indeed his pursuit of truth is such a long and varied one that no summary could do it anything like justice. For example, the constant comparisons between Yeats and Eliot tend to be unilluminating, and critics often fall into the trap of disparaging one to exalt the other. Professor Richard Ellmann has perhaps summarised Yeats as well as is possible, and has put sensibly the differences between Yeats and Eliot, though even here the disparagement of Eliot is unnecessary and unhelpful:

> In modern poetry Yeats and T. S. Eliot stand at opposite poles. For while both see life as incomplete, Eliot puts his faith in spiritual perfection, the ultimate conversion of sense to spirit. Yeats, on the other hand, stands with Michelangelo for 'profane perfection of mankind,' in which sense and spirit are fully and harmoniously exploited, and 'body is not bruised to pleasure soul.' So strongly does he hold this view that he projects sensuality into heaven to keep heaven from being ethereal and abstract. He presents this faith with such power and richness that Eliot's religion, in spite of its honesty and loftiness, is pale and infertile in comparison. . . . The principles of growth and of stability keep constant watch on one another in Yeats's poetry. He was a many-sided man who by dint of much questioning and inner turmoil achieved the right to speak with many voices and to know completely the incompleteness of life.   THE IDENTITY OF YEATS, pp. 246–7

The 20th century is big enough for at least two great poets, surely. The note of critical 'placing' and point-scoring is absent from a moving tribute paid to Yeats by a poet who has learned much from him, W. H. Auden. Auden, as Mr. John Bayley has pointed out in *The Romantic Survival*, uses a public symbolism in much the same way as Yeats, and he has, too, the same range of style and tone. This is the third and final section of Auden's *In Memory of W. B. Yeats*:

> Earth, receive an honoured guest:
> William Yeats is laid to rest.
> Let the Irish vessel lie
> Emptied of its poetry.
>
> In the nightmare of the dark
> All the dogs of Europe bark,
> And the living nations wait,
> Each sequestered in its hate;
>
> Intellectual disgrace
> Stares from every human face,
> And the seas of pity lie
> Locked and frozen in each eye.

Follow, poet, follow right
To the bottom of the night,
With your unconstraining voice
Still persuade us to rejoice;

With the farming of a verse
Make a vineyard of the curse,
Sing of human unsuccess
In a rapture of distress;

In the desert of the heart
Let the healing fountain start,
In the prison of his days
Teach the free man how to praise.

This magnificent tribute reflects Auden's awareness of the imminence of war in 1939, and expresses his sense of Yeats's supreme ability to experience and express the whole of life, and gain from the experience cause to rejoice in 'profane perfection of mankind'.

Finally, however, the experience of reading Yeats's poetry defies analysis or summary. Although he never achieves the sublimity of a Wordsworth or a Milton, his temptations and uncertainties make his poetry exciting in the way that the work of Donne or Blake or Keats is. His poetry makes us feel, to echo his tribute to Donne, 'that one who is but a man like us all has seen God'.

Appendix: Yeats at Work

The emotions of self-criticism and dissatisfaction with his own work are prominent in many of Yeats's poems. His poems often centre on the drama of his inner uncertainties. This self-criticism and dissatisfaction spring most frequently from his sense that he is simplifying experience or indulging in facile attitudes or expressions. The sense of necessary difficulty which he achieved as early as *Adam's Curse* never left him, and it acted as a constant safeguard against such characteristic Yeatsian temptations as those to escapism or rhetoric. This faculty for self-criticism is equally evident in the manuscript versions of his poems which have been made available by, most notably, Jon Stallworthy in *Between the Lines*. They provide further evidence of the truth of what he said in a letter to Fiona Macleod: 'I do so much of my work by the critical, rather than the imaginative faculty.'

Quite simply, Yeats was critical and suspicious of any perfect, timeless artifice, as, for example, the Byzantium poems clearly show, and it is therefore appropriate as well as revealing that as late as 1937 he was willing to change the opening lines of *Sailing to Byzantium* for ease of reading in a B.B.C. programme, to:

Old men should quit a country where the young
In one another's arms; birds in the trees . . .

This seems a good deal less urgent and dramatic than the original lines, so that one is glad that it never found its way into print; but on the whole Yeats's changes, both before and after publication, show a gradual improvement. There is the odd exception, however. It seems a pity that he discarded an early idea for the opening line of his epitaph in *Under Ben Bulben*: 'Draw rein;

draw breath.' This has a fine trenchant ring about it, and it seems possible that, had he lived, it might have been reinstated, as phrases which he had earlier discarded often were. On the whole, then, it is a very pleasant as well as rewarding experience to follow a Yeats poem through from his first inkling to the final version, and six poems of which interesting manuscript versions have been published show that his changes follow rather similar lines throughout his career: *The Sorrow of Love, The Second Coming, In Memory of Eva Gore-Booth and Con Markiewicz, Byzantium, An Acre of Grass* and *The Black Tower*. In what follows, the last version he reaches of any one stage of composition is presented without all the crossing out and insertion found in the actual manuscripts.

Yeats started *The Sorrow of Love* in October 1891, and the manuscript version quoted by Professor Ellmann in *The Identity of Yeats* shows the poem as Yeats originally conceived it:

> The quarrel of the sparrows in the eaves,
> The full round moon and the star-laden sky,
> The song of the ever-singing leaves,
> Had hushed away earth's old and weary cry.
>
> And then you came with those red mournful lips,
> And with you came the whole of the world's tears,
> And all the sorrow of her labouring ships,
> And all the burden of her million years.
>
> And now the angry sparrows in the eaves,
> The withered moon, the white stars in the sky,
> The wearisome loud chanting of the leaves,
> Are shaken with earth's old and weary cry.

Before its publication in 1892 this version underwent minor verbal changes to become:

> The quarrel of the sparrows in the eaves,
> The full round moon and the star-laden sky,
> And the loud song of the ever-singing leaves
> Had hid away earth's old and weary cry.

And then you came with those red mournful lips,
And with you came the whole of the world's tears,
And all the sorrows of her labouring ships,
And all the burden of her myriad years.

And now the sparrows warring in the eaves,
The crumbling moon, the white stars in the sky,
And the loud chanting of the unquiet leaves,
Are shaken with earth's old and weary cry.

The second version of lines 3 and 4 make the poem more logical
by using a verb that can apply to all three subjects, metaphoric-
ally at least. The change from 'million' to 'myriad' intensifies
the romantic aura of the presentation of the woman, and the
change from 'angry sparrows' to 'sparrows warring' produces
a more formal, loftier tone, as does 'unquiet' in line 11. Here the
tone of personal emotion is being submerged beneath a rather
self-consciously 'literary' diction. The final version of the poem,
as it appears in *Collected Poems*, was first published in *Early
Poems and Stories* of 1925:

The brawling of a sparrow in the eaves,
The brilliant moon and all the milky sky,
And all that famous harmony of leaves,
Had blotted out man's image and his cry.

A girl arose that had red mournful lips
And seemed the greatness of the world in tears,
Doomed like Odysseus and the labouring ships
And proud as Priam murdered with his peers;

Arose, and on the instant clamorous eaves,
A climbing moon upon an empty sky,
And all that lamentation of the leaves,
Could but compose man's image and his cry.

Technically and emotionally this is clearly superior to the earlier
versions because of its greater control and complexity. The
contrast between the first and last stanzas is managed much more
economically, being particularly striking in the antithesis between
'the milky sky' and 'an empty sky'. Again, the second stanza

manages to suggest universality through precise mythological references, which exploit specific associations, rather than through mere vagueness. The shattering of the veneer of comfort and complacency described in the first stanza is anticipated by the irony of 'that famous harmony of leaves', and the poem as a whole becomes great in a distinctively Yeatsian way in its suggestion that suffering has brought with it increased humanity, that an apparent loss is really a gain, positive 'composition' being preferable to negative 'blotting'. Here, certainly, Yeats's labours were rewarded, for the final version defines and clarifies what had been blurred and elusive.

The Second Coming, started in January 1919, has an interesting manuscript history in that the early versions show Yeats eradicating the merely topical from the poem, as well as cutting away verbiage. Thus the first draft exemplifies the poet's fears by references to the German advances in Russia in early 1918, and also contains references to Burke and Pitt. The first full draft, however, omits these references, and shows Yeats working particularly hard at the final lines. 'Rough beast' of the penultimate line occurred to him very late, and the drafts show 'has set', 'is slouching' and 'slouches' struggling for inclusion. The kind of inspired improvement Yeats achieved is shown by the substitution of 'rough beast' for the earlier 'wild thing', and of 'shadows of the indignant desert birds' for 'an angry crowd of desert birds'; and the verb 'reel', which combines so strikingly with 'indignant', came to him very late. What might have been a statement of fear in a particular situation becomes through revision a universal image of impending chaos.

In working from first ideas and drafts towards the finished poem, Yeats is also often concerned to cut away traces of over-explicit or over-intense bitterness, and this process is concisely illustrated in *In Memory of Eva Gore-Booth and Con Markiewicz*, where the finished poem has a poise and balance of recollected emotion very different from the tone of his first efforts. The poem was begun in the autumn of 1927. An early version of the first section reveals the basic impulse of the poem, Yeats's quarrel with Ireland. The girls are seen as martyrs to a worthless cause:

'But Ireland is a hag.' The drafts of this poem serve also to clarify the enigmatic elation of the concluding lines:

> Arise and bid me strike a match
> And strike another till time catch;
> Should the conflagration climb,
> Run till all the sages know.
> We the great gazebo built,
> They convicted us of guilt;
> Bid me strike a match and blow.

In an early version, the idea of striking matches goes with 'works of intellectual fire', produced by 'we that toil'. There is also a mention of 'widow Nature' who 'still/Has those cradles left to fill'. This is obscure enough, but the idea seems to be that Yeats and his fellow revolutionaries and writers inspired, kindled, the revolutionary movement which has now been overtaken by Time, but that this disappointment can be retrieved by further works of imaginative fire which can recreate a similar vision, another gazebo providing a view of the heroic possibilities these girls once embodied. Thus another early version of these lines is:

> And when the final embers gone
> Bid me let the sages know
> I the great gazebo built
> They brought home to me the guilt
> Bid me strike a match & blow.

Even when the last embers of the Irish Revolution are dead, there is still hope, though of a slightly different kind. This time Yeats —he is singled out in the 'I' of this version—will produce a work that will not be defeated by Time, nor tainted by guilt as political revolutions inevitably are. He will embody, in poems such as this, self-sufficient beauty and love which will defeat the enemy, Time. The 'I' of this version becomes 'we' only in the first printed version. The message of the poem might be said to be that, though 'Ireland is a hag' and has temporarily widowed Nature, Nature is always fertile, and needs only the love of Yeats and others of similar vision to defeat the ravages of Time and the stupidity of Ireland. If this is what the poem means, the drafts help to make the meaning more explicit, though, of course, this is not to say that the finished version is unintelligible. The meaning of the final lines communicates itself well enough, and certainly as poetry these lines are very much better than the early drafts just considered.

The early drafts of *Byzantium* show Yeats trying to make his meaning as explicit as the subject-matter allowed for the benefit of Sturge Moore, whose remarks had stimulated Yeats to write the poem. The first trace of the poem, which was written after a long and serious illness, is a note of April 1930: 'Describe Byzantium as it is in the system towards the end of the first Christian millennium. . . . A spiritual refinement and perfection amid a rigid world. . . . The divine born amidst natural decay.' The 'system' referred to here is, of course, that of *A Vision*, and this in itself makes the origins of the poem very different from *Sailing to Byzantium*. This poem begins with the aim of presenting and elaborating an idea through symbolism, whereas *Sailing to Byzantium* began, in its early drafts, with sardonic autobiographical reminiscence. The first draft of the first stanza contains a line which suggests that at this stage the idea of death as a necessary prelude to the experience of Byzantium was uppermost in his mind: 'When death like sleep has destroyed the harlot's song.' In his first attempt to present this stanza coherently he uses what was to be a key-word in the drafts, though not surviving to the final stage, 'intricacies':

> I tread the emperor's town,
> All my intricacies grown clear & sweet.

Although the poem is explicitly symbolic even at this early stage, it is also characteristically personal, and, as frequently happens, the first person pronoun appears in the drafts, though eradicated later: 'I tread the emperor's town.' Dissatisfied with what he has achieved so far, Yeats begins again, this time using in the opening line an image which is later subsumed into the magnificent conclusion, together with the echoed cathedral gong: 'All the tumultuous floods of day recede.' In the next stanza he begins to work at the presentation of the ghostly figure who is to act as his guide through Byzantium, and here the calculated ambiguity of the finished version is illuminated by the draft version:

> And I adore that mystery
> Harsh death in life, or that dear life in death.

'Harsh' and 'dear' spell out explicitly the dual aspect of this spiritual state, making it clear that Yeats is already aware of the dangers of excessive spirituality as well as those of excessive physicality. When he moves on to describe the golden bird of Byzantium, he is momentarily betrayed by his subconscious memories of Blake into:

> What mind decreed or hammer shaped the metal,
> Of golden.

This echo of *The Tiger* is emphatically crossed out. Moving on to the fourth stanza, the account of Byzantium's purgatorial powers of cleansing and purifying the newly-arrived spirits, Yeats tries two lines that are more explicit than the final version:

> All blood besotted spirits come
> And all that blood's imagination leave.

'Blood's imagination' is a fine phrase, and it is by no means obvious that the final version, 'complexities of fury', is an improvement. The earlier version achieves greater explicitness without any loss of literary power, and the repetition of 'blood' could be defended in itself, though perhaps not so easily in the context of the finished stanza with its three mentions of 'flame'. Not surprisingly, the highly complex concluding stanza troubled Yeats through several drafts, but it was the final lines that began to take shape first:

> Where blind images can yet
> Blinder images beget
> The Dolphin torn & gong tormented sea.

The emphasis on the 'blindness' of these stormy images, which is absent from the finished poem, is interesting, particularly in the light of this passage from *A Dialogue of Self and Soul*:

148

> I am content to live it all again,
> And yet again, if it be life to pitch
> Into the frog-spawn of a blind man's ditch,
> A blind man battering blind men;
> Or into that most fecund ditch of all,
> The folly that man does
> Or must suffer, if he woos
> A proud woman not kindred of his soul.

Here 'blind' is even more emphatically repeated, and its association with 'fecund' is thus stressed. The 'blind'/'fecund' association is equally important to an understanding of the concluding lines of *Byzantium* even though 'blinder images' of the draft becomes 'fresh images' in the finished poem. Though repulsed by art and spirit, these images are ultimately as irresistible as any basic life-force, and their victory is in little doubt. When Yeats begins a draft of the whole poem, he gets on fairly smoothly, if one can judge from the evidence of the manuscript. In the first stanza the first person pronoun is removed, again characteristically, but it is not until he reaches the final stanza that he makes any radical revisions. Working towards the final 'Marbles of the dancing floor/Break bitter furies of complexity', he tries:

> Integrity of the dancing floor; integrity
> Breaks the bleak glittering intricacies aimless flood of imagery.

'Integrity' is here used in its literal sense of 'wholeness' and the marked 'integrity'/'intricacy' contrast shows clearly what Yeats is describing, the conflict between the formal organisation of the world of spirit and art and the teeming multiplicity of the world of unshaped life. Even in the fair copy it is this final stanza that troubles him, and the fifth line in particular. In the draft for the printer, the importance of this stanza is emphasised by the change from 'These crowds approach' to the more dramatic and arresting 'Spirit after spirit!'

Yet another aspect of Yeats's complex character and difficult creative progress is revealed by the manuscript version of *An Acre of Grass*. Typically, it begins subjectively, though the first version is, in fact, remarkably similar to what eventually satisfied him. The most significant change is a characteristic one towards impersonality: 'My picture & books remain' becomes 'Picture and book remain', a change which reflects Yeats's habit of omitting the article to achieve verbal and emotional austerity. The second stanza seems to have been slightly harder going, though still not nearly as hard as in some of his other poems. The first attempt at the opening line, for example, is distinctly bad: 'Meditation is my temptation'. This he changes to 'My temptation is quiet', a change which, apart from producing a great literary improvement, shows clearly that 'quiet' is to be read as a noun in the final version rather than as an adjective. Stanza 3 seems to have come fairly easily, the only correction being from 'till' to 'that' in the second line, and indeed this correction is a technical one, simply reflecting the frequency of 'till' in the subsequent lines. Apart from punctuation—about which Yeats took very little care—the next stanza needed no revision. Further versions of the poem are found on carbon typescripts, and on the first of these there is a strange, overtly sexual, digression containing a woman's declaration of loyalty to 'Billy Boy'. In spite of knowing other men sexually, the woman says, she remains 'true to Billy Boy'. The digression, presumably an effort on Yeats's part to bolster his own sexual confidence, is clearly related to the theme of the poem, a refusal to grow old gracefully and quietly, but poetically it is of little worth and it is not even bawdily funny. On the second carbon copy a more profitable change, which finds a place in the finished poem, can be seen. The poem as typed is, at this point:

> My temptation is quiet
> Now life's end draws near
> Neither loose reverie
> Nor those thoughts that hear
> Dry bone grind dry bone
> Can make the truth known.

Crossing out all but the first and last lines, Yeats wrote at the side of these lines the very different final version:

> Here at life's end
> Neither loose imagination
> Nor the mill of the mind
> Consuming its rag & bone.

The appropriately Blakian image of 'the mill of the mind' is a triumph of Yeats's method of composition, and 'rag and bone' (to be used again in *The Circus Animals' Desertion*) is so much more telling than 'Dry bone grind dry bone'.

The last poem Yeats wrote, *The Black Tower* of January 1939, obviously did not receive the painstaking revisions given to the earlier poems, but it did undergo considerable changes. Rather like *Leda and the Swan*, it seems to have begun as an explicitly political poem, this time concerned with Irish resistance to English influences and hope of a future victory over the traditional enemy. Yeats was a dying man when he began the poem and so the first efforts in particular are very confused, but the first full draft, *The Old Tower*, which is in prose, clearly presents the poet himself as the speaker. This version also shows that the poem is essentially very similar to *The Gyres*, containing Yeats's optimism about a future resurgence of Ireland as the gyres progress: 'I speak for the gyres of the black tower.' The gyres reference, though it does not survive long, is the key to the meaning of the finished poem. In an early version of the poem's refrain, there is a reference to the heroic dead of Ireland and to the battle of the Black Pig of Irish legend in which the English enemy were to be finally crushed:

> Our fathers stand among the rocks
> But winds can the old bones shake
> When it cold blows from the black pig's dike.

Another interesting fragment among the early manuscript versions of the poem is an incoherent passage on impending death, apparently addressed to his son, but even when his own death was so obviously very close Yeats took care to see that this intensely personal section did not appear in the finished poem. Before writing a draft of the complete poem, Yeats introduces a character called Old Tom, the cook, who 'swears he has heard our master's horn', though the speaker of the poem says: 'But I think he's a lying hound.' In the first composite draft of the poem Old Tom is no longer given his proper name, becoming simply 'the tower's old cook'. The cook, as he appears in the finished poem, is a typical Yeatsian character for the reader is left in uncertainty as to whether some revelation is at hand or whether what the cook says he hears is mere self-delusion. The men of the black tower are torn between Time and Eternity, and their uncertainty is more explicit in an early draft's 'I think he's a lying hound' than in the final version, 'But he's a lying hound'. One final point about Yeats's revision of this poem serves to illustrate the heroic discipline of his art. Even in the face of death he refuses to make his poem just a receptacle for personal fear; he still strives towards the universal statement, changing the line— 'And there in the tomb we stand there upright'—to the comparatively detached: 'There in the tomb stand the dead upright.'

In fact, if any valid generalisation can be made about the directions Yeats pursues in his manuscripts it is that he tends to cut away the autobiographical element and the references to personal friends and contemporary events from which his poems often have their origin. This is not just modesty; it is part of his anxiety to be understood, to make his poems more than embellishments on his personal life. Apart from this, of course, since he was a first-rate craftsman, his work on his drafts almost always produces a literary improvement. Most of all, however, his labour at his poems, before and after publication, testifies to his constant development, and to his two basic, sometimes conflicting, beliefs: in the power of poetry and in the irresistible demands of life's flux and complexity.

Reading List

1. TEXTS

The Collected Poems of W. B. Yeats (Macmillan, Second Edition, 1950).

The Collected Plays of W. B. Yeats (Macmillan, Second Edition, 1952).

A Variorum Edition of the Poems of W. B. Yeats, edited by P. Allt and R. K. Alspach (Macmillan, New York, 1957).

A Variorum Edition of the Plays of W. B. Yeats, edited by R. K. Alspach (Macmillan, 1966).

(These variorum editions record all the different printed versions of Yeats's poems and plays, showing very clearly his constant dissatisfaction with his own work.)

Autobiographies (Macmillan, 1956).

Essays and Introductions (Macmillan, 1961).

The Letters of W. B. Yeats, edited by A. Wade (Hart-Davis, 1954).

Letters on Poetry from W. B. Yeats to Dorothy Wellesley (Oxford University Press, 1940).

Memoirs, edited by Denis Donoghue (Macmillan, 1972).

The Senate Speeches of W. B. Yeats, edited by D. R. Pearce (Faber and Faber, 1961).

Uncollected Prose: First Reviews and Articles 1886–96, collected and edited by John P. Frayne (Macmillan, 1970).

A Vision (Macmillan, Second Edition, 1937).

2. BIOGRAPHIES

Hone, Joseph, *W. B. Yeats, 1865–1939* (Macmillan, 1942).

Jeffares, A. Norman, *W. B. Yeats, Man and Poet* (Routledge and Kegan Paul, 1949).

3. CRITICAL COLLECTIONS

Cowell, Raymond, *Critics on Yeats* (Allen and Unwin, 1971).

Donoghue, D., and Mulryne, J. R. (eds.), *An Honoured Guest* (Arnold, 1965).

Garab, A. M., *Beyond Byzantium; The Last Phase of Yeats's Career*, (Northern Illinois University Press, 1969).

Gordon, D. J., and others, *W. B. Yeats, Images of a Poet* (Manchester University Press, 1961).

Jeffares, A. Norman, and Cross, K. G. W. (eds.), *In Excited Reverie* (Macmillan, 1965).

Maxwell, D. E. S., and Bushrui, S. B. (eds.), *W. B. Yeats, 1865–1965* (Ibadan University Press, 1965).

Unterecker, John (ed.), *Yeats. A Collection of Critical Essays* (Prentice-Hall, New Jersey, 1963).

4. CRITICAL BOOKS

Bloom, Harold, *Yeats* (Oxford University Press, 1970).

Ellmann, Richard, *Yeats, The Man and the Masks* (Macmillan, 1949).

Ellmann, Richard, *The Identity of Yeats* (Macmillan, 1954).

Henn, T. R., *The Lonely Tower* (Methuen, 1950).

Jeffares, A. Norman, *W. B. Yeats. The Poems* (Arnold, 1961).

Koch, Vivienne, *W. B. Yeats. The Tragic Phase* (Routledge and Kegan Paul, 1951).

Melchiori, Giorgio, *The Whole Mystery of Art* (Routledge and Kegan Paul, 1960).

Parkinson, T., *W. B. Yeats, Self-Critic* (Berkeley, University of California Press, 1951).

Parkinson, T., *W. B. Yeats, The Later Poetry* (Berkeley, University of California Press, 1964).

Rudd, M., *Divided Image* (Routledge and Kegan Paul, 1953).

Stallworthy, Jon, *Between the Lines* (Clarendon Press, 1963).

Stallworthy, Jon *Vision and Revision in Yeats's Last Poems* (Oxford University Press, 1969).

Stock, A. G., *W. B. Yeats. His Poetry and Thought* (Cambridge University Press, 1961).

Ure, Peter, *Yeats the Playwright* (Routledge and Kegan Paul, 1963).

Ure, Peter, *Yeats* (Oliver and Boyd, 1963).

Wilson, F. A. C., *Yeat's Iconography* (Gollancz, 1960).

Wilson, F. A. C., *W. B. Yeats and Tradition* (Gollancz, 1958).

5. ESSAYS ON YEATS

These books have interesting chapters on Yeats:

Kermode, Frank, *Romantic Image* (Routledge and Kegan Paul, 1957).

Stead, C. K., *The New Poetic* (Hutchinson, 1964).

Wilson, Edmund, *Axel's Castle* (Scribner, New York, 1931).

6. THE BACKGROUND

Kirby, Sheelah, *The Yeats Country* (Dolmen Press, Dublin, 1962).

Inglis, Brian, *The Story of Ireland* (Faber and Faber, 1956).

Kain, R. M., *Dublin in the Age of W. B. Yeats and James Joyce* (University of Oklahoma Press, 1962).

All the books mentioned make an important contribution to the understanding and appreciation of Yeats, but, after reading the poetry, the student fresh to Yeats could not do better than begin with Joseph Hone's biography. Of the critical works, Professor A. G. Stock's book is probably the most lucid.

7. RECORDS

W. B. Yeats, Siobhan McKenna, Micheal MacLiammoir, *The Poems of William Butler Yeats* (Spoken Arts, 753). The first three tracks are of Yeats reading his own poetry and prose.

Siobhan McKenna and Cyril Cusack, *The Poetry of Yeats* (Caedmon Literary Series, TC 1081).

The Caedmon Treasury of Modern Poets Reading their Own Poetry (Caedmon Literary Series, TC 1995). Yeats reads three of his own poems on this record.

Micheal MacLiammoir, *Ireland Free, Revolutionary Speeches and Poems of Ireland* (Spoken Arts, 749).

Index